CW01310186

Samuel Pepys
An Edinburgh Town Dweller's Christmas Chronicles 1971-1996

Like his more famous London namesake, Edinburgh's Samuel Pepys kept diaries and journals as well as also being a public servant for a goodly number of years.

The cover photograph is of the Royal Mile after heavy snow from February 1996, photographer unknown. Most of the illustrations are taken from old postcards or Christmas cards. Every effort has been made to trace and acknowledge copyrights: any oversights will be rectified by the author immediately.

Samuel Pepys
An Edinburgh Town Dweller's Christmas Chronicles 1971-1996

'In the bleak midwinter
Frosty wind made moan
Earth stood hard as iron
Water like a stone
Snow had fallen
Snow on snow on snow
In the bleak midwinter
Long, long ago...'

Christina Rossetti

Preface

The Christmas Chronicles tells the story of day to day life and what it was like to spend Christmas and New Year in Scotland's capital during the decades of the 1970s, 1980s; and 1990s. The extracts are based on the Samuel's diaries and journals taken from between the start of the winter solstice on the 21st December through to twelfth night come the 6th of January.

With the passage of time – it's almost half a century since the schoolboy entries were written in 1971 they now offer a certain period charm capturing day to day life in the lead up to the Festive holidays through to New Year ending on twelfth night. The posts take the form of a Dali folded clock so that although the diary extracts correlate with each day in December and January they include entries from over 25 years so Samuel appears as a boy, as a youth and as a man - as a schoolboy or at work - single or married - as a son, an uncle and eventually as a father too.

It's rather like a TV soap spread across three decades from which a tapestry begins to be weaved and distinct characters emerge of a family encompassing great-grandparents; sets of grandparents; aunt; mother; father, brother and sister and many others too who flit in and out of the family story over the Yuletide holiday.

The journals begin in 1971 when Samuel is a 14 year old Boroughmuir schoolboy through to him approaching middle age when he celebrates his 40th birthday in 1996 and leaves the capital to move to the Highlands. The chronicles are set within the social culture of Edinburgh and include entries on sport; the arts; newspapers; books; radio; and television as well as the city's shops and the surrounding landscape and of course the ever present and varying temperamental Edinburgh climate and weather. Whilst much of the story is about the author and how he views the world, a flavour of that time, that place and that era is captured – a capital Yuletide tale - a local Christmas story, but a universal one too.

Yuletide

. . . tried to warm himself at the candle

Birth: *'the coming into existence of something'.*

In the bleak mid-winter, Dickens' Christmas stories give the reader images of hope and light; warmth and joy; as well as transformation and resurrection. However, the light is tempered by the darkness and cold too which makes it even more life enhancing. The hope comes from spring, surely following winter and the renewal of life as Scrooge is restored to the good values of his boyhood and youth.

Six decades ago in the deep mid-winter of 1958, the Hanlon family moved into the newly built Edinburgh Corporation flats at 6 Oxgangs Avenue to take up residence at the Stair; Charlie and Hilda were full of hope at the beginning of the exciting adventure ahead and novelty of bringing up their family in a new home. Like the other young families at 'The Stair' they had their dreams and aspirations of the good life and raising their children as well as they could, with all the fun, joys and worries inherent.

At this time, only Michael, the eldest brother had been born; he would only have been around one year old; Brian, Colin and Alan would come along in the following years. When the family took up their tenancy at 6/7, like the other seven families in residence they were issued with a rent book. It records their rent as being eighteen shillings a week. Most remarkably, Hilda, the last remaining original resident at the Stair, still has the family's first rent book. It records their date of entry as 15th December 1958.

In a way the document records the birth of The Stair when one of the original inhabitants first took up residence there and is perhaps a unique document of its type. Brian speaks humorously about the family's first experience. Hilda recalls how the Pepys family had already moved in downstairs to 6/2 slightly earlier. The coal-man was delivering coal to our family - Ken and Anne Pepys, the author (Samuel aged two) and my brother, Yohanan (aged only a month). Hilda wanted to buy some coal in too, to heat their new home.

However the coal merchant turned down her request as she lived on the top floor and he mustn't have fancied walking up another three flights of stairs. Given it was mid-winter and Michael, the eldest brother, was still only a baby, the stone-hearted coal-man clearly wasn't full of the Christmas spirit. He reminds me of Ebenezer Scrooge to Bob Cratchit, that '...there will be no coal burned in this office today...'

Hilda must have found a way forward, not only to heat their new top flat home with its fantastic views to the hills and to the sea, as well as to the prominent Edinburgh Castle because she and Charlie went on to successfully raise their four boys in a happy household, throughout the decades of the 1960s and 1970s.

Spring and indeed summer followed winter.

In the years and decade of the 1960s that followed, at this time of the seasonal year, my sister Áine, brother Yohanan and I, whatever our circumstances found that come Christmas, 'Santa Claus' always did us proud. Christmas was always the best and most exciting time of the year for us. When I say Santa (aka Mother, sometimes with support from Father) did us proud, I don't mean that we were spoiled or received any expensive presents; indeed, quite the contrary. And instead, we each received a stocking which was filled chockfull of imaginative small presents which were an absolute delight to wake up to on Christmas morning.

Like most children it was the one evening in the year when we were keen to go to bed early of our own accord. And of course it was the one winter's morning in the year that we were keen to get up early too!

I'm not too sure how Christmas worked in all the other households in the Stair. But, perhaps only Norman Stewart at 6/3 did better than any of the other children in terms of expensive presents. But where we did get a small insight into how the season was celebrated within other homes was on our return to school in January. The teacher always asked each of us individually to tell the rest of the class about our main present. Well, we hadn't really received such a thing from Santa; instead it was just small, charming little serendipities. I therefore didn't enjoy this and I can recall telling a fib saying that I had been given a graphic designer's set. Of course I didn't have a 'scooby' what that was but I was determined not to be out-gunned by Norman; being an immediate neighbour and friend, he of course was the one pupil in the class who knew perfectly well that I had not received any such thing!

In my mind's eye Christmas Eve was always a very quiet evening in the Stair. I recall Father going out on several Christmas Eves to attend the local Watchnight church service, presumably at Colinton Mains Parish Church, the same church which the Swansons, our immediate neighbours at 6/2 attended. Although we could hear the church bell ring out at St John's Church up the hill, I don't think Father went to the remarkable Reverend Jack Orr's service.

Over the years our mother and Mrs Molly Swanson had a reciprocal arrangement whereby Mother gave Gavin and Heather Swanson a wee tin of Woolworths' toffees each, whilst we children each received something from Molly and Dougal. On one memorable Christmas I received a 'book' from her, but when I opened it, rather than pages, much to my delight, it instead contained seven tubes of sweets arranged horizontally inside.

The three Hogg girls up above at 6/3 always received 'girly pressies' and I can recall my sister Áine spending time with Christina, Maureen and Eileen at this time of the year. I'm vaguer on how the Blades at 6/6 spent Christmas, other than when Alison, Ruth and Esther Blades could be seen out playing, bouncing around on their new Spacehoppers which were introduced to the United Kingdom in 1969.

Before Áine was born our grandfather gave Yohanan and me a bobble Santa each which were full of wrapped toffees. The Santa figure is delightful and has been carefully looked after these past fifty years; and each year we bring them down from the attic to be displayed. The Swansons also received a similar Santa figure too but they had less jolly faces.

The Hanlons and the Blades often hung linked paper ring decorations in their living rooms which reached from corner to corner across the ceiling. I used to regret that we were more conservative with only our individual Woolworths' decorations on display. Today I appreciate how attractive and aesthetically pleasing they are. However there wasn't the same crowded and crude effect, which as a young boy I naturally liked and preferred. I suspect Woolworths did Mother and many other parents proud over the decades.

On going to bed on Christmas Eve each of the three of us would leave one of Mother's nylon stockings at the foot of our beds. In the early morning I was always the first of us to awake. I would crawl down to the foot of the bed and reach out to see if Santa had arrived - YES! - Oh the excitement of feeling the bulkiness of the misshapen stocking full of surprises - it was the most wonderful sensation in the world! 'It's Christmas! I would bellow out. 'It's Christmas!' I would shout, as I jumped down from the top bunk bed to the floor to switch on the bedroom light and awaken the others.

The stockings were quite wonderful and filled with torches; little games; Yogi Bear or Huckleberry Hound picture books; perhaps a young person's novel; colouring books and pens; a selection box; some gold coins; an orange and an apple and a half crown; and the obligatory Broons or Oor Wullie annual in later years.

Áine meanwhile would get some 'girly stuff'. I particularly recall a delightful peach smelling cream. Yohanan might receive a toy car, perhaps a Corgi or some Matchbox cars. On one occasion when quite young I got a leather football and football boots - the first boy in the immediate neighbourhood to receive such sports items; however it was the old fashioned heavy leather ball and big unwieldy boots too which would have taken a Messi to able to control the ball with.

In our innocence we would then rush through to awaken our parents to show them what 'Santa' had brought us! These Christmas mornings were simple little affairs, but wonderful. No matter how poor we might be, Mother ensured that these were magical occasions every year for us, from being very small children right through and into our teens; happy times and very very sweet memories which I've never forgotten.

Christmas Day was rather like Sundays, only quieter. We saw very little of what went on in the rest of the Stair because our grandfather would collect us all mid-morning in his large Ford Zephyr car with its leather bench seats and drive us all down to Portobello for the day not returning us back home to Oxgangs until late in the evening.

We always spent the whole day at our grandparents' home at Durham Road, Portobello. I therefore have no intimate knowledge of how the Swansons; the Stewarts; the Hoggs; the Smiths; the Blades; the Hanlons; or the Duffys spent their Christmas Day. However, Christmas Day is the most popular church day of the year, so I could surmise that the Swansons probably attended Colinton Mains Parish Church of Scotland; meanwhile, the Blades will have gone along to one of the Baptist churches; whilst the Duffys will have celebrated Christ's birth at St Marks Roman Catholic Church, Oxgangs Avenue.

The drive from Oxgangs down to Portobello from the Stair was always the quietest of the whole year. Sundays were normally quiet, but on Christmas Day there were even fewer cars on the road and we just sailed down as if we were the Royal Family. We drove through Greenbank, Morningside and along Grange Road and on through the Queen's Park passing Duddingston Loch on the right, always looking out for the 'skating minister' as we assumed it was his home! And on the bad bend outside the 12th century Duddingston Kirk our grandfather always blared the car's horn loudly, impishly hoping it was midway through the chaplain's sermon. We then wended our way down to Joan's and the excitement of turning right at the foot of Durham Road with its fine small Edwardian mansion-houses.

It was our grandmother who made Christmas the day that it was. She would be there on the doorstep to greet and welcome us into the hallway and we would give her a formal light kiss on the cheek.

Although she loved us all very dearly she wasn't effusive and instead had more of the demeanour of a conservative English gentlewoman's restraint. And instead she expressed her great love for family and many others through innumerable acts of kindness over the years and the decades.

The hall looked resplendent. There would be a flower arrangement on a dark antique table and for once the royal blue carpet had been hoovered clean. As a busy artist, jeweller, pottery decorator, lace-maker and gardener our grandmother didn't want to be remembered for dusting the house; instead she had far more important priorities, but Christmas was an exception. And because her house resembled 'The Old Curiosity Shop', full of fascinating antiques and interesting items from throughout the world the hall really didn't need any Christmas décor. Although, I suppose one could have hung some tinsel from the African buffalo's antlers high on one wall! In later years I lived there from the winter of 1972 and whenever I invited a friend, a colleague or a journalist into her front room, their first comment on entering was always 'What a fascinating room this is!'

Apart from the tiny kitchen, her house was perfect to host the large Christmas gatherings which took place there for over half a century. The hatch linking the kitchen to the sitting room was a clever little idea. As the kitchen had no work space or work tops at all, the Buchan's pottery casseroles containing hot vegetables were placed there and also delicately balanced on top of the old washing machine.

Grandma Joan had the most wonderful grace under pressure; I never saw her get flustered. Indeed, when I think about it, I never recall her raising her voice in all the subsequent years that I stayed with her. The only hint of any colourful language emanating from the kitchen would be from Father working hard as he whipped the cream by hand. Our grandmother served up those wonderful

Christmas dinners through the magic little hatch, year in and year out, until she was well into her eighties when I took over hosting Christmas as the 'Laird 'o Plewlands'; then at West Mill, Colinton; and for a few years in The Northlands.

The first course was usually home-made soup. This was followed by the traditional roast turkey; mashed and roasted potatoes; various vegetables; and two types of stuffing - sage and onion and sausage-meat all served up with gravy. And despite being a butcher our grandfather never carved the bird and instead that too was also left to our grandmother; she was very much the matriarch.

The dining table was lovely to behold. With the eye of the trained artist the table was laid out with colourful antiques and glassware. It looked like something out of a Dickens novel. There would also be beer, lemonade and as we children got older, the excitement of having some Woodpeckers Cider too. Around the table the craic was good; some teasing - some wit - some awful jokes - pulling crackers and several of us cajoling our grandmother to 'Come on through Joan and enjoy your dinner too!' Atypically, she was always the last to take a seat at the table and join the extended family.

There were various puddings - trifles, a mix of milk and water jellies and single, double and whipped cream. However, before we could face our pudding, we children would often go outside into the winter air and stroll around the back garden to help regain our appetites.

Grandma Joan always prepared a home-made Christmas plum pudding and we children would 'ooh and aah' when the brandy was poured on top of it and lit. The flame puffed up almost taking our eyebrows off. To accompany the pudding there was both custard and ice cream, the latter coming from either the wonderful Arcari's, Portobello or Lucas, Musselburgh, Italian ice cream shops which served Edinburgh residents so well over the years.

Because of the large number of people around the old dining table - the very young; the young; adults; the middle aged; the old; and the very old, those occasions were quite magical throughout the decade of the 1960s. The age range of those sitting around the table covered approximately ninety years thus stretching back to when Queen Victoria was on the throne. Sometimes there might be a dozen or so of us present. Was it Old Aunt Mary or our great-grandmother, Wee Nana, who always said 'Now, Joan, where's the silver spoon - you know I can't possibly eat my pudding without it!' And, when I was very young, her husband, 'The miser' aka Pumpa (our great-grandfather) tried to slip me a penny, which I turned down, much to his amusement!

Once Christmas Dinner was over and before the Queen came on the television to broadcast to the nation, the adults would retire

gratefully to various rooms throughout the house to allow their food to digest. Mother would enjoy a snooze in one of the bedrooms, usually my grandmother's south facing room, which always had a very comforting and quiet feel to it. Meanwhile, Aunt Dottle would be in the kitchen with her sleeves rolled up, washing dishes in the sink, often with Father giving her a helping hand. Others would find a spot on a spare sofa, put their feet up and place their head on a soft cushion and shortly be happily asleep. Meanwhile, we children might go out to the garden. It was good to go out with Yohanan from the warmth of the house and in to the fresh cold air in the winter garden. We enjoyed having a blether about our presents or kicking a ball around.

The bare winter December garden had a completely different feel to July when it was lush and adorned in its summer clothes. In its hibernated state all that remained were the skeletons and structures of trees, hedges and shrubs. And, as the afternoon coolness descended, and the light began to disappear, I enjoyed the quiet and solitude of the garden and the slightly brooding presence of the season. All that separated the light from the dark, the cold from the warmth, was a solitary door.

It made me think of some lines from Buchan's 'The Power-House' where the hero, Sir Edward Leithen, is told: 'You think that a wall as solid as the earth separates civilisation from barbarism. I tell you the division is a thread, a sheet of glass. A touch here, a push there, and you bring back the reign of Saturn.' And then, it was braw to go back into the warmth of the house and the bosom of the family and to be reminded once again, that it was still Christmas Day!

After the Queen's broadcast a highlight for me was to sit quietly in the smoking room at the front of the house. This was the front room, which was fascinating and relaxing to be in because it was full of antiques, paintings, glassware, snuff bottles and old French clocks.

I sat on the big old sofa alongside my grandfather, whilst my great grandfather and father sat on the large squishy chairs opposite.

There was a large old gramophone-come radio cabinet in the corner and a Christmas tree in the bay window. It was here that the men retired to enjoy the home-made sweets which our grandmother made annually for Christmas - marzipan and walnuts; peppermint creams; fudge et al. But most of all I liked when the men enjoyed a cigar. I loved the smell of the cigar smoke. It's a smell which immediately transports me back through the mists of time.

I loved sitting quietly, listening to my great-grandfather, grandfather and father talking and conversing. I always kept very quiet and tried not to be intrusive in case I wasn't allowed to stay.

And, as the light began to slowly fade and darkness fell and the street-lights flickered on outside, we switched the Christmas tree lights on. The lights were a novelty as we didn't have them back at The Stair at Oxgangs. And in that room, surrounded by three older generations, I felt part of a line going back to Victorian times. I also felt warm, secure and at peace. I didn't want these moments to end and savoured the hour or two before someone would look around the door to say that 'Tea was now being served and would the men come through and join the rest of the party.'

We would all troop through to enjoy some fresh cut bread, salad and some John West salmon which was a luxury item back in the 1960s. There would also be a variety of shortbread, Christmas cake, mincemeat pies and for the gutsy perhaps seconds of trifle and cream. By then a good fire was blazing in the grate and one of the nice things about Christmas Day compared to our Sunday visitations was that we got to stay on a little longer into the evening.

Our grandfather would give our great-grandparents a lift back home to London Road, Dalkeith, before then returning the seven or so miles back to Portobello to give the Pepys's a lift back home to Oxgangs Avenue and The Stair.

On the way home to Oxgangs in the car, we would all snuggle up together to keep warm. However, unlike the journey down, which was taken in the eager anticipation of a family Christmas Day, moving towards its zenith in the bright winter sunshine, come the end of this most special of days, it was now appropriately dark, as Christmas began to die its death.

Now passing Duddingston Loch to our left it was so black out that we couldn't really see the loch unless the moon was out and reflected upon its surface, dancing on the dark waters. And this in contrast to a century before when Robert Louis Stevenson enjoyed the season and wrote in the winter of 1874 of looking down upon the skaters on the frozen loch flitting around under the light from the moon and the lit torches.

On leaving the Queens Park, we children reverted back to playing a game to see who could count the most lit Christmas trees in sitting room windows along Dalkeith Road, Causewayside, Grange Road, Morningside and Greenbank, before we descended into Oxgangs.

And then, of a sudden, we were back from where we'd started out.

It was of course a stark contrast coming home to The Stair and 6/2.

The house was quiet. It was cold. And the one bar electric fire would be immediately switched on. However, it was slightly more inviting than usual, because the Christmas tree decorated the corner of the living room and we had the pleasure of coming back home to our presents. And before going off to bed I would carefully re-pack my stocking with my presents and place it at the end of my bed to try to recreate the Christmas morning experience when I awoke on Boxing Day.

However, it was never the same.

'The Advent wind begins to stir
With sea-like sounds in our Scotch fir,
It's dark at breakfast, dark at tea,
And in between we only see
Clouds hurrying across the sky
And rain-wet roads the wind blows dry
And branches bending to the gale
Against great skies all silver pale
The world seems travelling into space,
And travelling at a faster pace
Than in the leisured summer weather
When we and it sit out together,
For now we feel the world spin round
On some momentous journey bound -
Journey to what? to whom? to where?
The Advent bells call out 'Prepare,
Your world is journeying to the birth
Of God made Man for us on earth...'

John Betjeman

Prologue

7th October 1990 Colinton Edinburgh was a lot quieter with the rain. I was in at Jenners' Christmas shop buying in some little charms for Martha's Christmas pudding. Delightful! I had to telephone both her and Janey from the store to check they were both prepared to fork out £9.99 each for them. It felt a lovely moment to be standing there in the shop soaked in my big coat speaking to them sitting in our farmhouse kitchen back at West Mill where they were baking both a cake and the pudding together. How our life has changed since moving there in mid-summer. Thereafter I looked into the old country shop in Cockburn Street and bought some silver threepences as a present for Martha.

17th October 1982 Portobello To Jenners' Christmas shop - thoughts? I'll have to think about that one. Their china shop however is marvellous. Looking around it appreciating the finery of the pieces makes me understand now why Margaret Ross has so loved collecting such items over the years. We received some free chocolate from a Ritter girl inducing me to treat myself to a bar priced at 44p. It rained a bit. On now to George Street and to a smallish 'affair' (Book Fair) at the Assembly Rooms where I picked up two books. We sat in enjoying a coffee and a roll. I wonder if that old lady ever won her flight around Edinburgh. I do hope so. We walked down Frederick Street to St Stephen's Street and on to Stockbridge. It's such a lovely area with the lit shop windows full of interest. It's a joy to saunter along on either side looking into this window and that one. The whole area is so full of atmosphere all enhanced with it being a mid-autumn overcast Edinburgh day. And of course, Saturdays are best and most magical of all.

23rd October 1993 Colinton Earlier in the morning Martha and I drove into town to a curiosity shop in Cockburn Street to buy some silver threepences for the Christmas pudding which Martha was making today.

16th November

1980 Portobello A windy day and a shock as I made my way along Portobello Promenade to come across a good-looking Jaguar car in the sea! Evidently some bloke had been putting his boat in the water not quite appreciating how quickly the tide was coming in. The car had been left overnight. I bought the new Neil Diamond album before going down to the West End to meet my father and step-brother. I thought how very lovely Binns' Christmas window looked.

1981 Portobello This morning I got back into a new-old routine again – the messages and some running of course, but with more of a purpose. On the Durham Avenue runs I was able to gauge my fitness: although the times were slower I'm confident of swiftly getting back to the pre-Highlands holiday fitness. Now that I'm back in the capital I'm quite enjoying myself. Joan was in good form talking about yesterday's (Sunday) Edinburgh Mineral Club social and asking me about our holiday. The house had a lovely warm feel to it today with a good going coal fire and perhaps just the merest hint of Christmas in the air. I thought how well the front room looks: Joan has obviously been busy and it's full of plants brought in for the winter although Martha says the bulbs will never be out come Christmas, but only time will tell. Twas a busy afternoon looking down to the library, The Dole and into CAB before doing a training session on the school brae. Just as dusk was falling I stood in Portobello Park for a quarter of an hour just taking it all in – the late autumnal air with winter fast encroaching whilst I reflected on life thinking about everything that's good about it and where it might yet go: the street lights were flickering on and the first of the workers' cars were heading down Milton Road West with their headlamps lighting their way. And all the while I enjoyed simply standing there in the parkland alone, a part of it all yet apart from it all with the endorphins from the session enhancing the moment. I walked up to the bus stop to meet Martha at the top of the road: she was surprised and delighted to see me thoroughly approving of me wearing the large Arran sweater. We spent most of the evening through in the front room with Martha studying by a corner lamp next to the electric fire with me opposite compiling a diary index, supping a sherry. She says that I've 'delusions of grandeur'. Dinosaurs on the box followed by bed.

1982 Portobello I spent the morning at home working on my Countryside essay: after lunch just as I was arriving Mother and Spieler arrived. I attended an afternoon lecture out at Cramond before meeting Martha in town. The rain poured down. We wandered around. Jenners' Christmas area looked lovely. We bumped into Ann Forbes: she told us Paul was through in Glasgow for a recording of Allan Wells on *This Is Your Life*. Home for a big tea.

17th November 1983 Portobello Sitting here in the front room first thing I thought there was just the merest hint of Christmas. The room is cold and crisp. Two boxes of biscuits in their Christmas tins nestle on a chair. It reminds me that Martha said last week that she intends travelling north come the 25th December. That hurts me. I'm aware of and fully understand the difference between the joy she'll get being at home again with her family as opposed to spending it with me. I guess it's where she sees her priorities lying on that day of all days. I met her for lunch. The urge to see her and to meet up just came in to my mind so I called her. She took me along to the Sik Tek Fok for a pleasant wee lunch – a lovely interlude in the day. It was rather good fun, the gradual gleaning of information from each other as to how we've been spending our days apart. It was like a chess match. Slowly we were both able to form a picture of where we're both coming from – our thoughts – our feelings – our doings. Fencing, but without swords! Later on I wandered around the shops enjoying a bar of chocolate. In the evening I managed to grab a lift out to Oxgangs with Áine and Spieler. They were showing some slides so I just disappeared up to Lee's. I stayed there all evening. I sensed a difference with him confirmed by a Freudian Slip that I was manipulating him – Julie, no doubt at work! However, as the evening wore on and the conversation improved it actually ended up being a fun evening, especially on the moral maze topic of whether one should forget to forgive. I said No. Lee – and his book! – said Yes.

19th November 1981 Portobello Martha was nervous about this morning's Stock Exchange exam so she was keen for me to accompany her to the examination hall. We were early so had a coffee at the West End. After seeing the poor lass to the door I left her to wander around a few shops. Mum was down at lunchtime and as a graduation present has given me the second volume of Historic South Edinburgh by Charles Smith which will bring ongoing pleasure especially as this volume contains chapters on Hunters Tryst, Swanston, Comiston and Greenbank. Martha and I enjoyed a lovely Thursday late evening shopping out in town. She'd done her best in the exam – if she's failed it will be because it will be down to poor organisation and assistance from Wood-Mackenzie. We met at The Assembly Rooms to take in the

Charities Hypermarket. The items represented excellent value for money all served up nicely by the blue rinse set late middle-aged ladies serving their passage to heaven! On now to Marks and then to Jenners with the evening's highlight being their Christmas tree. It's immensely tall and decorated with yellow, red, blue and white lights with a star on the top. We walked along Princes Street to Debenhams - the quality of goods are fine but the prices a bit rich, but that said it's good to have another large store in the capital. Thereafter we enjoyed getting back home to Porty for a meal by a lovely warm glowing fire whilst outside it sounded a little stormy.

20th November

1979 Portobello Overnight there was an exceptionally heavy frost. Whilst out for an early morning run and when running past Brighton Park, oh for a camera - there was a nun walking, appearing to be floating, across the frosted park grass - she was heading in early to the St John the Evangelist's Roman Catholic Church.

1981 Portobello The weather was very poor today. It was bitterly cold and damp with showers and on top of that there was an absolute hurricane a-blowing as witnessed by the astonishingly quick times as I did a session down Durham Avenue. It was as if I had a sail on my back as I was swept along by the force of the wind. Thereafter it was the usual busy active sort of a day including a visit down to Portobello. Come four o'clock I took a bus out to Oxgangs but not before stopping off at the Christmas Hypermarket at George Street. The town was cold too with a bitter wind cutting straight through me. At Oxgangs Yohanan, Áine and Mum were a bit out of sorts, at least until I arrived livening up the scene. The 'duchess' lay reclined on the sofa resting during the daylight hours to the dismay of her children who had all arrived home starving. But with me as the catalyst Yohanan and Áine soon both bucked up somewhat. I arrived back at Portobello to catch Martha lying naked in the bath - very well timed! We enjoyed a relaxed Friday evening in. I've started reading *Anna Karenina* - a cracking long novel with me getting off to a very good start with it.

1982 Portobello We spent all morning (Saturday) looking at the Christmas goods in the shops but didn't buy much other than emerging with some cards, labels and tape. It was quite cold out. In the afternoon I worked for a couple of hours on my Countryside essay. The evening's TV was excellent – *The Count of Monte Cristo* followed by the first episode of *Shogun*.

23rd November 1993 Colinton More snow fell in the Dalkeith area this morn and in the afternoon too. Resting on the tree branches I thought how beautiful it looked. I thought too how noble the many horses looked that I passed standing in the fields with their gentle faces bearing the brunt of the weather with their usual quiet stoicism. I drove down to Sam Burns's Yard at Prestonpans to buy a chest of drawers for the baby. Because it's solid oak it's £45. Still, just consider what we might have paid at Pine Country, etc. An evening in. The Health Visitor called round – damage limitation – she had goofed after leaving a very public message for Martha at her work saying the ante-natal class was cancelled - Martha is yet to inform her work thus far that she's pregnant! More snow fell in the Dalkeith area this morn and in the afternoon too. Resting on the tree branches I thought how beautiful it looked. I thought too how noble the many horses that I passed looked standing in the fields with their gentle faces bearing the brunt of the weather with their usual quiet stoicism.

24th November 1982 Portobello I was going to have gone into Dunfermline College of P.E. this morning but Martha thought it would have been daft to only use the car for the few lit hours of the afternoon. We collected our hired car outside the Caledonian Hotel – it was a brand new Ford Sierra – what a beautiful car to drive. We set off for the Borders shortly after ten o'clock shortly after taking Joan to Dodge City. I felt sorry at Martha taking fright that she had left the keys in the car. But fortunately the boot was open! Martha drove us down to Melrose past occasionally flooded roads. The Pentlands were quite magnificent covered in snow whilst on the lowland areas there was nothing to be seen. I don't recall seeing such a contrast before. At Melrose we enjoyed lunch in an old fashioned hotel in the town square. There was a lovely open coal fire on the go with some old colonel type figures in their tweeds etc. Twas another world altogether. We enjoyed a good greedy lunch – pizza and chips followed by gateaux. We travelled back to Edinburgh via Peebles. We stopped for afternoon tea up at the chair-lift at Hillend: the slopes were busy with many skiers out enjoying sailing down the hill. They served up nice hot drinks and home-made biscuits. We took 'the boys' – Bruce and his friend Robert - up to the chair-lift. They were surprised at both the cold, but also the wonderful views of the city on the ride back down.

27th November

1983 Powderhall It was rather pleasant to be so very ordinary joining Martha and many of the capital's citizens for a Saturday morning up town just floating about. Opposite our bus stop there was a Christmas Fair at the church. It was only 10p to get in. Martha bought a toast rack and some satsumas. I bought a book or two. It was fun - a fun time in our young lives playing at being a couple. At George Street at The Edinburgh Bookshop we bought some books for our nephews - my selections were *Noggin of the Nogs* and *Captain Pugwash*. We broke for lunch at the Rose Street Brewery: it's rather attractive with an old English inn feel to it with filling fayre too - steak pie. Later, Martha bought some Christmas handkerchiefs at Jenners - a tradition going back to her grandmother's time. My sister Áine served us.

1984 Powderhall It was a funny sort of a day at work. Despite trying I didn't seem to achieve a lot. The day itself simply flew by. Of course there were big moves on with the word processor. Martin and some of the girls have moved on to the first floor. And at lunchtime I was out for two hours spent mainly in the Second Edition Bookshop where I picked up an illustrated copy of The Beloved Vagabond - I may give it to Joan for her Christmas.

28th November

1980 Portobello Snow! At 6:15 a.m. Radio Forth said it was minus 3. On the way out to college on the 34 bus travelling up The Royal Mile the snow came tumbling down. The street scene was quite breath-taking. What with Edinburgh's skyline, the grey sky and the lights from the cars and the shops we could have gone back in time and it could just as easily be the 1940s or my favourite, the 1950s. I loved it! However no snow lay. College was fine and I studied in the library until three o'clock. Come the evening I sat in going over an old Law paper and watching the box.

1981 Portobello (Martha's writing) *Martha was first out for a run this morning - sprinting from the postbox to the bus stop.* She was at Queen Street this morning working overtime until one o'clock. I had a busy morning. First of all I wrote out 1000 words before proceeding to do a hill session on School Brae. It was a sharp morning out. Once back to the house I completed Yohanan's birthday cake putting on the chocolate butter icing inside the cake and then the frosted chocolate icing exterior. Just as I was leaving to meet Martha up town Yohanan happened to give me a buzz. Martha and I spent a lovely Saturday afternoon up in Edinburgh. We walked down to Stockbridge picking up a baked potato enroute. We darted in and out of several shops. Stockbridge is so much more pleasant than the over-crowded Princes Street: it's so full of character. Late afternoon we took a 29 bus up to Marchmont and from there walked across to Church Hill and down Morningside. We looked into Studio One – they had one or two nice things especially in the Christmas sweets line. By now it was 4:30 p.m. and dark and cold so we caught a 5 bus home. Martha felt a tad sick for a short while but soon recovered. Meanwhile Aunt Dottle is down with a bug. 8 months into our relationship things are rather wonderful between Martha and myself and I thought I should record just how happy I am. Oh, some good news – Margaret has proposed that she and Joan take a trip to London and also to Florence no less!

1985 Powderhall A lovely photograph awaited at Duddingston Loch which was frozen over, with birds walking on the surface and the sun reflecting off the ice: meanwhile a family or two fed the ducks.

1993 Colinton A very pleasant Sunday. I looked into town very briefly to do a little Christmas reconnaissance but no joy. I trained up at a coldish breezy Campbell Park. Meanwhile Martha baked a cake which we took down to Yohanan for his birthday to his cosy Duddingston Village flat. A pre-birthday tea all enhanced with Mum and the girls along and Áine later. I ended up entertaining the girls for ages before Martha and I left to go to the beautiful Advent Service. I'm not religious but I enjoyed the Carol Service at St Mary's Cathedral at Palmerston Place. With the candles burning inside, the cathedral looked beautiful – twas quite meditative. Outside it was cold, with a biting wind chill factor – one degree, but with a high wind a-blowing.

1994 Colinton Another Monday and an ever-increasing workload. I'm very much looking forward to my break over Christmas – yahoo! I looked into Joan 's at lunchtime. Aunt Dottle was there. She had gone over on her ankle. Joan said how she quite fancied going off for a run in the car. I fancied it too but unfortunately had to return to work! Martha bought a rather nice chair this evening from a nearby house.

1995 Colinton I was awoken during the night by Martha - bad flu, headaches and shivers. On one occasion I also awoke from a strange dream. I was high in the gods - a theatre rather than say a church - I was attending my own funeral. From up above I was looking down and watched my coffin being carried away - surprisingly there was a good turnout! - Yohanan looked rather sad - I shouted down to him, something along the lines of *'I'm alright mate!'* - it was eerie - then, the next thing I knew I'd turfed somebody over the balcony - I then escaped down the stairs and went out through a side exit and jumped into a waiting car, however unfortunately the lights were at red, and with people starting to close in, I tried to remain calm before the lights changed and I belted away before I awoke.

30th November 1981 Portobello It rained and rained this morning. We got soaked on the way to Martha's work. I ran back from Church Hill. It was quite cold too - hardly surprising with the start of winter tomorrow. Joan wasn't feeling 100% and and neither was Aunt Dottle who was under the weather and off work today. Mum phoned them to see how they were doing remarking how Yohanan had embarrassed Áine in front of Thomas. In the afternoon I trained up at Meadowbank with Cameron Sharp. I enjoy talking with him. I stayed with him for most of the session but my legs were a tad dead on the last few repetitions. Afterwards he gave me a lift up to Queen Street in his M.G. - it's very small with the windscreen terribly close to your face, but it's nice enough although I prefer the (Triumph) Spitfire. Martha and I picked up an Advent Calendar - isn't it exciting - the start of December tomorrow and the Christmas countdown. We spent the evening inside by the fire - plus a bath.

1st December

1984 Powderhall We'd enjoyed ourselves last Saturday at the Freebody's waitress service Victorian Restaurant at Debenhams so we decided to repeat the experience this morning. Once again we greatly enjoyed ourselves, beautifully looked after by the young girls serving up our teas, coffees, and whipped cream, scones and jam and cakes. The simple things in life with Joan being able to escape to the town once a week. Martha told me off afterwards for speaking too much to my grandmother leaving her with Aunt Dottle. I was telling Joan I'm keen to collect illustrated books by Dulac and Rackham. After leaving everyone I went off to West Port Books: the Rackham illustrated copy of *A Christmas Carol* was no longer in the cabinet. My heart sank. However it turned out to be there and the owner, Bert Barrott, sold it to me for £25. I snapped it up. I'm to be (partly) reimbursed by Mum and Áine. I was also pleased to get a copy of John Masefield's *The Midnight Folk* for only 50p. I think it's interesting. I telephoned Joan in the evening: she was bubbling over saying she intends giving me the Red Cross book illustrated by Dulac as my Christmas present: I told her you better not as my mother has informed me (today) that she's picked it out for herself! I caught Yohanan out at Oxgangs for ten minutes. I told him that his birthday and Christmas present is a set of driving lessons. Come six o'clock I picked up a Chinese carry out for Martha and me. I thought we were going to go halfers: instead she thanked me for it: I didn't say anything!

1994 Colinton Whilst out for my early morning run I thought of the James Taylor song and the first line 'The first of December...' There was a frost out and also a mist come fog in the lower lying areas, however I was flying along nicely. At the City Hospital a fox ran across my path. This morning I had a big blow-out with my boss, His Nibs over my job evaluation. He just can't help himself in personalising things. I managed home at lunchtime mainly because I didn't see Wee Atticus last evening as I'd taken Joan and Aunt Dottle up and back to the Edinburgh Sketching Club. On the return journey from Great King Street to Portobello I gave Joan a tour of the capital's Christmas Lights which she enjoyed.

2nd December 1995 Colinton I oversaw the Christmas Lights switch on at Penicuik, Loanhead, Bonnyrigg and then Dalkeith where Runrig's Donnie Munro (an Eskbank resident) made a most eloquent speech on the festive season of the year and the importance of a sense of community.

3rd December

1993 Colinton It's the end of the working week although I'm out tomorrow overseeing the Christmas Lights Switch-On Ceremonies throughout Midlothian Martha telephoned to say she had got on quite well at the GP and had decided to go into work but would take it easy. In the morning I met with Strategic Development about my job evaluation. They commented that it was well-presented and were optimistic. I now await His Nibs getting out the red pen! I saw Dr Broadwood. He wonders if it might be scabies. On to the next treatment.

1994 Colinton It was the first occasion for a while that the four of us – Lee; John; Yohanan and I - were out playing golf at Vogrie. It was a good and unusual match with 8 of the 9 holes being won with the match going to the last. We'd arranged to play on the Saturday morning as I was working in the afternoon - it's that time of the year again organising the four Midlothian Christmas lights switch on ceremonies. The morning was mixed with some showers and just as we finished off the round there was a very overcast sky. In the afternoon five of the family were out this year to watch the Christmas Lights Switch-On Ceremonies. Martha and Atticus were with me here in Dalkeith although Atticus was asleep when the lights were switched on. Councillor Sam Campbell was loving his high profile role. My heart was aflutter for a moment - there was a six or seven second delay after he pressed the bell before the lights came on! We travelled home to Colinton via the lights at Bonnyrigg and Loanhead: our lights are old fashioned, but all the better for that.

4th December

1976 Portobello My cold is worse and I felt poorly. Spur of the moment I built a snowman out in the garden which might produce a smile or two from passing neighbours. I looked out to Oxgangs. Yohanan's motorbike had broken down at Meggetland so we towed it back over and across the ice - what a laugh! The snow has been continuous since 10:30 p.m. last evening.

1980 Portobello I was out doing some exercise early this morn as I'd intended going into college early for what I hope turns out to be a worthwhile Economics lecture. I didn't fancy a steady run so instead did something locally. Today was much more disciplined in all departments scoring myself a healthy 95%. I studied a bit. My sister Áine called at lunchtime so I looked out to Oxgangs in the evening to give her a wee hand with an educational assignment. Lee and I cheered Yohanan up with a jar up at The Good Companions. I got home late, taking a 27 bus to Princes Street: the Christmas lights were lovely with the beautiful Norwegian tree on The Mound and the floodlit castle as a backdrop. Oh! – last evening a 'mummy' was found in a wardrobe in Durham Road! It was a dead woman's body in the queer sort of a chap's house up the road on the opposite side.

(**Note:** His mother had died earlier on and the poor chap took fright or else didn't wish to lose her and had perhaps simply panicked storing her body in a cupboard in the house. The chap was clearly unwell with mental health issues. For years you might see him occasionally walking the short distance up Durham Road to collect a few groceries. He had lank light brown greased back hair and summer and winter always wore an old stained white raincoat that had seen better days. At the time he would have been in perhaps his mid-40s. He always seemed to have a leer or half grin on his face. His was an unsettling presence. Because he lived on the opposite side of Durham Road, if I ever saw him it was usually from across the road on the opposite pavement. I think he lived on his own with his mother. After the drama of the event he may have been hospitalised for a period of time before being able to return to live on his own there. At one stage before he was hit by mental illness he perhaps cut the image of a dashing gentleman about town because in his garage there was an old M.G. sports-car of perhaps post World War vintage.)

1981 Portobello I tried something different this morning. I clearly need to do one long run a week, perhaps for around an hour, so, for the first time I took it very very easy indeed – all that's really required is to keep the heart and lungs - the general system ticking over for an around an hour. I found that I quite enjoyed myself reflecting that if I kept that simple pace going for the length of a marathon I could do so if I so wished. Whilst out in The Meadows I bumped into an immaculate looking Charles Blades – a man alone, poor beggar. I spent a quiet hour in town including buying *Songs of a Sourdough* (Robert Service) for only 50p. At four o'clock by accident I bumped into Paul so we hung around till our prospectives arrived out of work. This Friday evening was the first occasion that I had seen the capital's Christmas lights – they're very lovely. Martha wasn't pleased with our graduation photographs especially as a proud Joan was taking them up to this evening's Edinburgh Mineral Club. But the two of us rather enjoyed going along to the Aladdin's Cave (Safeways) for the messages. With all the seasonal serendipities in the store it's always a smashing time of the year to go shopping. Coming to the end of our first year, well 8 or 9 months together, we're very much a team. After her bath Martha roasted chestnuts on the fire for the two of us - mmmh!

1984 Powderhall I meant to say yesterday that the blue tits have discovered the coconut I put out on the balcony of my Grosvenor Crescent office.

1991 Colinton A cold frosty day. I had a half day. Yohanan and I tidied up much of the cherry tree which we sawed down on Saturday past. I'll return Margaret's chainsaw in the next day or two. Biffo is on a cushion in front of me on the table as I sit writing my journal. His brother, that beggar Fearty, got a long-tailed tit today. On Monday past we went through (to Glasgow) to watch Nanci Griffiths in concert.

1993 Colinton First thing this morning I replanted lots of daffodils in tubs and pots. Thereafter I looked in to the record fair picking up stuff alongside some Christmas presents too. I looked into Bargain Books. I feel guilty about spending so much money especially with a baby coming along but I couldn't resist buying a copy of Leonard Woolf's Letters reduced from £16 to £6. In the afternoon I was at Dalkeith for the Christmas Lights Switch-On Ceremony. It went okay albeit after a few alcoholic drinks a councillor began complaining! Lucille joined us in the evening for a Chinese with Desi joining us at 10:00 p.m. Come midnight I sat and watched the BaaBaa's against New Zealand.

5th December

1971 Oxgangs I enjoyed another good game of football. It's really great that the weather is holding fine now we're in to winter. Once you get running about nothing could be finer than playing. Being a Sunday and with it getting dark quite early on I settled in for an evening in front of the telly. BBC in its prime with another televised classic. I've been following *Tom Brown's Schooldays* for the past month. It's absolutely fantastic with the beastly Flashman as Mum calls him - the Beeb hasn't been holding back with some sadistic scenes but no worse than getting six of the belt off the Hunters Tryst headmaster or Mr Rush at Boroughmuir. I read in the newspaper that Mrs Mary Whitehouse hasn't been too amused. Later on we switched over to STV to watch the cool Paul Newman in *The Moving Target* - like Tom Brown it was fantastic but very different

- Newman was ace. I'm just going off to bed now - a new week awaits.

1994 Colinton (Danderhall 10:00 a.m.) There was a new start at work today - Catherine Airth. She's interesting - pleasant, but with a coolness to her too and a tough edge too all combined with a natural instinctive intelligence. She has her work colleague, Alison, well sussed already! November was autumn, December really is winter. The temperature has dropped significantly. This evening the wind blew and the rains came down. I drove Nell home - she'd come round for the evening. I lay in bed thinking of a remark she'd made about how her mother had loved Christmas when the three kids were around (herself, and two brothers, one of whom who alas died years before in a car crash) and how she would have wished to have that time back again. Now of course, in the main, she spends her evenings alone. Áine, Yohanan and I too had some good fun too. Earlier on I was on the phone to Áine for half an hour.

1995 Colinton Winter has arrived early this year - we're only five days into the season and there's already much snow in the south of England. Whilst putting in a training session in the gloaming up at Campbell Park we had a slight flurry. I enjoy being outdoors in such conditions, almost alone, other than the odd person or small group out with their dogs. Later I did a few weights in the garden shed at the foot of the garden with the temperature gauge registering zero. I lay on the sofa watching the football while Martha and our bairny snoozed whilst I delight in the joy they bring me. I'm continuing to enjoy Sereny's biography of Speer reading it into the early morning hours. Earlier I dropped a copy of *A Christmas Carol* off to Yohanan to read - most appropriate for him at this time of the year and it's heavily illustrated too. What a sight at lunchtime - 87 year old Joan trying to get into her long-johns! Earlier I dropped A Christmas Carol off to Yohanan to read - most appropriate for him at this time of the year and it's heavily illustrated too.

6th December

1991 Colinton 6:00 p.m. It's Friday evening now but I'm working tomorrow - it's the Christmas Lights Switch On Ceremonies throughout Midlothian at Penicuik; Loanhead; Bonnyrigg; and Dalkeith. I'll also pop out on Sunday to Newbattle Pool to put in an appearance at the swimming championships. Later this evening at 8:00 p.m. I'm playing football down at Portobello with the MDC (Midlothian District Council) crowd. I also played yesterday lunchtime out at Lasswade. Last evening I took Joan up to the Edinburgh Sketching Club crit night – between dropping her off and picking her up at Great King Street I looked into Waterstones Bookshop – a nice innovation in the Edinburgh cultural scene. Earlier I'd dropped in at three o'clock for an egg and bacon tea – I'd been in the area picking up some radios – walkie-talkies for the Christmas ceremonies - so it was convenient to do so. Last night Martha was out too doing late night shopping picking up some duvets for the spare room. And the new sofas arrive next Monday so we're getting there.

1993 Colinton After only five hours sleep, for a Sunday I was up early. I went into town in the morning picking up some Christmas cards. Come lunchtime I joined Adrian for a session up at Campbell Park. He reckons that my skin disorder emanates from the large graze on my right leg. I think I picked it up in the garden whilst putting the trellis up 4 or 5 weeks back. In the afternoon Mum, John, Caomhog and Lulu looked round for afternoon tea – exhausting! John put up Robert's tray! (Robert was a dumb waiter!)

7th December 1973 Portobello Darby had the car back which was good. At half past the flaming snow started and it came storming down for the whole day. It was about four inches thick and even the corporation buses had stopped running. I've decided to give Marion the Comp (Thomas Graham & Sons Ltd. Builders & Plumbers Merchants 51 Balcarres Street Morningside) and Joan two weeks' monies so that I can get new shoes next week. I met Darby at Cluny Avenue where he always parks the car across from James Waugh & Son Butcher's. He wandered across to the car watching how he went in the snow wrapped snuggly under his cap and in his tweed jacket and a parcel under his arm. Darby went nice and slowly coming home tonight particularly through Arthurs Seat which was pretty bad. His watch-words on foot, when driving the car and in life is *Gang-ginger!* I didn't go up to Meadowbank this evening sitting in front of the coal fire watching the telly.

1981 Portobello I did a long steady run this morning through The Grassmarket, the Meadows, and Arthurs Seat. High up on the top road through Holyrood Park was a joy running easily after forty minutes with the air crisp and fresh and the view down on to Duddingston Loch and the village: a wonderful feeling. Martha called at lunchtime. She was glad she'd gone into work and was feeling not too badly. I told her to take it easy. In the afternoon I went up to Meadowbank and trained on my own. It was so bitterly cold I didn't do a lot. I also spoke to Bill Walker for a quarter of an hour about my training before going up to Queen Street to meet Martha after work. She didn't think I'd make it so it was a nice surprise for her. A relaxed evening in reading and...and...

1982 Portobello Twas the heaviest frost of the winter. At six o'clock Steven and I ran up to Duddingston Village. It was actually good fun passing along the streets, the houses and the town and village gardens all a Christmassy white. I saw Martha to her bus before spending another few hours on this final essay of the term. I've more or less finished it but I feel it's a tad weak in parts and overall it's too descriptive and not analytical enough. I arrived out at Cramond in time to join our wee group for the lunchtime run. Come mid-afternoon the weather changed considerably – stormy even with high winds and a heavy rain. Quite a dramatic change from first thing this morning. I looked into Meadowbank but only to do a circuit. It was a pity I hadn't arrived earlier as the group doing a session would have suited me as I could have handled them easily. And then home to enjoy some leisure reading rather than academic tomes. Martha meanwhile is out with Sealbhaigh. I've picked up where I left off with (Leon) Edell's *Bloomsbury – A House of Lions* – excellent!

1987 Morningside 9:30 p.m. It was the coldest evening of the winter. I was taken by surprise at just how cold it was when I was out for a run in the evening. My ears were tingling. The pavements were icy. The weather man says it's minus ten around Aviemore with Edinburgh at minus two. In the afternoon I played Lee at snooker winning 2-1. Like my golf I'm a much improved player. Earlier I'd purchased Martha's present to me – a 2nd edition of John Buchan's *Scholar Gypsies* – it's identical to the first edition. The morning was taken up with a meeting out at Penicuik. I enjoyed my weekend and being away from work. Saturday was spent in town including lunch at Helios Fountain with Martha and Lucille: thereafter I wandered off on my own. In the evening I was snug in by the fire with plenty of scran. On Sunday I joined the big group for an enjoyable long run along the Water of Leith.

1990 Colinton Outside it's snowing – the first of the winter. There wasn't an enormous amount but neither is it small. I was taken by surprise when I drew back the West Mill curtains. It's Biff and Fearty's first experience of it. Last evening I drove Joan and AUNT DOTTLE up to the Edinburgh Sketching Club at Great King Street. I also took Mum home from Áine's. I managed to train yesterday but four weeks in I've still got catarrh, rubbish in my chest, etc.

1992 Colinton 11:00 p.m. I had a half day today. I walked round a wet but mild Edinburgh doing some Christmas shopping. Joan was under the weather and had spent the morning resting in bed. I looked in briefly at lunchtime. Aunt Dottle had taken the day off work. Yesterday (Sunday) I cleared out the gutters, planted four senocia plants, put up some shelves in the hut, tidied the house, put up some punchy covers, etc. Martha arrived back from the Highlands in an irritable, unhappy mood – she was sobbing.

1994 Colinton It was another raw day. I took Atticus down to Colinton before spending the day (Wednesday) in town, somewhat unsuccessfully a-searching for Christmas presents. Thereafter I was quite disciplined tackling an albeit easier track session at Arthurs Seat especially given I was tired from walking around Edinburgh and hungry too. Helen and Lexi had been down from Perth with Atticus evidently behaving badly! Martha had felt bad about Robbie and Helen spending a lot of money on a car seat which will do Atticus for the next couple of years.

1995 Colinton Martha remarked that whilst Atticus had been a little clingy at the playgroup today it was very encouraging and pleasing to see he was keen to help and become involved when they were setting out the chairs and tables. He is galloping along – only single words – but his understanding is excellent. This evening he even allowed me to put him to bed whilst he was still awake. Come teatime Martha was straight out into Edinburgh to do some Thursday late evening Christmas shopping.

8th December

1972 Oxgangs With Christmas just over a few weeks away I got a lift into town at lunchtime with the warehouse manager Iain Slater. I managed to buy a few family presents. I also looked into Jeffrey's Audio House at Bread Street and bought two new singles including

What Made Milwaukee Famous by Rod Stewart. With it being a Friday and the end of the working week I went up to Oxgangs at 5 p.m. to visit Mum, Áine and Yohanan. Then it was back down to Porty with Darby. Friday night's treat night so we had a fish supper from St Andrew's Restaurant. They must be the best in town.

1988 Morningside The Plewlands Terrace Morningside sitting room has been transformed and looking rather lovely since the tiled 'Victorian' fireplace was installed and the surrounding mantelpiece adorned with Christmas cards and bits 'n bobs and our tree standing proudly in the bay window. Martha returned to work today. Much to my relief the documentation has come through for a temporary overdraft for the fireplace. Yesterday I paid £170 for a Coia sketch of the ballet dancer Rudolf Nureyev – don't tell Martha!

1995 Colinton There was a heavy frost that didn't lift all day long. There was snow on the Pentlands and with the sun shining above them the view from the Rosewell-Peebles road across the snow-dusted countryside was quite wonderful. I finished work early to allow the three of us to go into town to buy the past year's special issue stamps for Atticus: I'd like to build up an album of such stamps in the years ahead – indeed all such issues since his birth last year.

9th December 1984 Powderhall Today was to be a tough day as I had two exams to see through so I was up at 5:30 a.m. to study. I was shocked to hear the news that John Lennon was shot dead in New York last night – an absolute tragedy for a man who has brought so much pleasure to millions – so senseless. The exams went well – Economics in the morning – Law in the afternoon. I spent the evening relaxing – studying and a bit of the box.

10th December

1981 Portobello There was a light as light can be sprinkling of snow this morning – only 10 seconds worth but with the heavy frost it turned everything into a romantic white, like a frosting on a card or a cake. As for the front room I remain convinced the Snow Queen resides there overnight because the windows were completely covered in a thick frost and ice with the most beautiful and quite incredible patterns. You could neither see out nor in the windows. John was down giving me a hand with the chimney: a fair amount of soot came down. I'd have preferred to do the job with Martha though. At lunchtime I jogged and had a shower up at Meadowbank. Mum was down giving me £4 for the photograph. At teatime in the early evening I trained with Paul. Despite the cold – it was very white out with a covering of frost – a very crisp winter's evening - we ran a decent 600 metres; I was only a second back so it was quite pleasing – thereafter we ran half a dozen 150s. I enjoyed the session. We had a lot of fun too with a good few laughs along the way. He's incredibly fit just now. And then home. To where the heart is and Martha. Supper and then a relaxed evening in together. She'd managed to successfully pick up several Christmas presents up town after work – Thursday late-night shopping. She wrapped up Lucille's present. Aunt Dottle's gifted me one of her bottles of home-made wine to take to tomorrow evening's dinner – very good of her. Boy is it cold.

1982 Portobello It's.....SNOWING! I jogged up Durham Road at six o'clock. It was difficult to run as it was quite slushy: Steven thought so too so I just went back to bed, but then I thought, look I'm up - the hardest part on a dark winter morn – let's do something. So I ran up to the (Duddingston) village and back. I looked out to Dunfermline College of P.E. and had a wee game of pool, some lunch and then a swim in the pool. Thereafter I looked into town before heading home. With it being Friday it was Safeways. And that's about it. So went the day.

1994 Colinton A wet Saturday morn but the weather didn't prevent us heading down with Joan and Aunt Dottle to Peebles for our final visitation of 1994. We kicked off with the usual pleasant coffee and scones at Kickers? Thereafter we spent our usual 90 minutes a-wandering around the shops: Martha picked up a copy of *The Black Tulip* for our collection. In the afternoon I looked after Atticus with a little rugby on in the background whilst Martha headed down to The Gyle - in between she looked back with an eight foot tree for Christmas.

11th December

1971 Oxgangs The last day of the working week. It's funny the way I'm relatively disciplined making sure the 'mail gets through' on dark winter mornings yet I can't seem to attend the school during the hours of daylight. Although I could have asked them to chum me I just left Ali, Paul and Yohanan asleep and joined the Blades on the early morning number 16 bus down to Morningside. As ever the paper round was fine on a Saturday, the best day of the week for them and I was happy to pick up my wages too. After breakfast Lee, Yohanan and I headed off for a day in town and had a pretty good time. We wandered about Princes Street to the shops including stopping off at Woolies and having juice and chips in their cafe. Afterward we crossed Princes Street to go to the Carnival at Waverley Market where we had a brilliant time. We were on quite a few of the rides including the waltzers and dodgem cars. I like some of the games - particularly the hoopla stall. It looks dead easy to throw a wooden ring over a ten bob note or a quid but it's harder than it looks. I also love the slot horse racing Derby game. Although it's good fun you have to keep your wits and Oxgangs street-sense about you as there's always Neds wandering about so there's a mix of fun and danger. A relaxed evening back at 6/2 doing nothing although Joan and Darby were out - good to see them.

1981 Portobello An early Friday morning struggling along but still with the energy to take in some magical surroundings: the Meadows were crisp and white and then from high up on Arthurs Seat I looked out and down upon Prestonfield House and out toward the Pentland Hills beyond and then to my left Duddingston Village nestling into the hillside all set within an amazing white mistiness. I did the messages alone at Safeways this morning rather enjoying myself although it was a pain to have to wait for a 5 bus for half an hour on the way home. A leisurely afternoon reading (Peter) Alliss followed by a hot bath before going up to meet Martha by the Christmas tree at Queen Street at six o'clock. As we walked along to the Two Inns for a drink it was windy and cold. I espied Gavin Miller en-route – he didn't look 100%. We had a drink which went straight to Martha's head! I managed to pick up a small bag of goodies for her – a roll and a small tart to help counteract the effect. We then went out to Lucille's for a meal – chicken, rice and cabbage. I rather enjoyed it. The evening itself was fine – nothing outstanding but it drifted along on the right note which was different to what I might have expected as Martha had pr-warned me that Lucille can be unpopular with some people by being a little aggressive. However, I found no real sign of that. Walking down a white-white Durham Road late at night hand in hand with my lover I felt wonderfully happy.

1982 Portobello Is Saturday the first day of the student holidays or is it Monday? Whilst it was nippy there was no frost. I looked into a small Portobello book sale – twas unfortunate there was nothing as the books were priced at only 10p each – I bought a couple of Ian Hay's but no Maurice Walsh's as Joan has them. I trained quite well and hard – come the end of the session I was stiff as a board – my legs were flooded with lactic acid leaving them feeling like rigor mortis all over. I joined Martha back home for lunch. She had been having a quiet-cum-busy morning not wishing to venture up to the crowded Saturday town today. She'd ironed, cooked baked potatoes and made coleslaw. Lovely! After lunch we walked down to Portobello which was quite busy with a Santa in his Grotto with the mums and kids all in a line. There was a Christmas Fair at Portobello Town Hall so we popped in for a few minutes with Martha commenting on the pleasant ambience. I picked up *The Roadmender* for 10p as well as some treacle, bread and dates for the Christmas pudding followed by tea and coffee at a delightful little shop called The Tea Cosy – dainty, with tables and all rather pleasant. Come the evening I read E.M. Forster's *The Longest Journey* but I found it difficult to really get into it. And then *Shogun* on the box and then.....

1983 Powderhall It's nine o'clock in the evening and I'm not looking forward to returning to work tomorrow morning – I've that Monday morning feeling on Sunday evening – it's the prospect of returning back to the world of Bob Cratchit and the great accounts books of the (Scottish Episcopal) church. Of a sudden it hit me two hours ago as I put my donkey jacket on to leave Lee's. I've only been employed there for around ten days and there's already a feeling of alienation - being un-creative - the boring repetition - and the thought that here I am a-wasting the precious hours and precious days of my life. It was perhaps also a reaction to spending an enjoyable 24 hours with Lee. As ever we enjoy each other's company – talking, laughing and also enjoying the silences too. I dragged him out of his pit at 9:30 a.m. for a run up Craiglockhart Hill. In the City Hospital grounds he tripped over a tree root. I roared with laughter. He almost didn't bother getting up again. He walked to the top complaining about his lungs – three months ago he was able to run all the way, but all this laying around has caught up with him. But on a crisp winter Sunday morning I enjoyed having his company out and about. Later on I had a short but highly amusing chat with Julie (his mum) about homosexuals and what they get up to together with Lee all the while giving practical demonstrations in the background! I looked into Mum's for an hour. She wasn't the cheeriest – her washing machine has broken down. Coming home to Dunedin Street on the bus just outside Jenners the first snowflakes began to fall. The church bells were ringing out. The Christmas town lights were a-shining. But still, I felt low.

1985 Powderhall I dropped Martha off at Queen Street at work at 10:30 a.m. and then went down to Meadowbank joining (Dave) Campbell's squad. It was okay but my Achilles heel was sore, indeed both of them were. After joining Joan for Sunday lunch I collected Martha. We wandered around a few shops before going down to Stockbridge for an ice cream and to buy a few Christmas decorations. The weather is damp and mild. In the evening I looked into Lee's and watched a James Bond film but he, Jimmy, etc were all but dead.

12th December

1981 Portobello We spent a lovely Saturday up town including Jenners, Marks and John Lewis's where Martha bought a game for Roddy, a wallet for her father, Wyvis and a photograph frame for Nell. We picked up a hamburger roll and chips eating it sitting on a cold step in Thistle Street. At four o'clock we took the dog down to the Figgate Park. The pond was heavily frozen over with figures darting here and there some of whom were good skaters. We had a lot of fun throwing the ball and the dog chasing it: twas like something out of a Disney film watching the dog as she tried to come to a halt retrieving it in her mouth. It was really very funny watching her skidding about all over. And then of a sudden DISASTER struck as Jill (the Fox Terrier) fell through a hole in the ice – panic stations! God! She got the shock of her life. She struggled to scamper out which she only did with Martha's assistance as she bobbed about in the icy water. It had the potential to have ended in tragedy. Anyway we managed to smuggle her back into the house to get her dried before Joan saw her. She seems to be no worse for her experience. We spent the evening in front of the coal fire with Joan before walking down to Porty to St Andrew's Restaurant for a fish supper.

1983 Powderhall On the crisp early morning run there was a light smattering of snow on some Edinburgh streets whereas other parts were dry and clear and others still covered in a thick ice. Charlotte, I mean St Andrew's Square had the best covering of snow followed by the banks of the Water of Leith which I traversed later on on my cycle to work. I had to gang ginger looking out for icy patches. At work, good and bad news awaited: the heating wasn't on and we were told if it didn't reach 60 degrees by ten o'clock we could all go home for the day. Unbelievably at five to ten the damn thing (heating) came on so we were asked to report back after lunch. It would have been lovely to have the whole day, but I guess we're never happy. I therefore went for a game of snooker, but with no money I had to cycle along to Ferranti's to get some from Yohanan who managed to scrape enough together. He was in a Monday Mood. Lee rattled up a bite to eat – chips, beans and toast – not bad at all. The afternoon slipped gently by. I was somewhat embarrassed when Mr Mackenzie insisted on paying for my staff Christmas lunch - £11. I eventually accepted because he was so insistent – I guess with me only starting recently and having not received a salary he wanted to be helpful. I feel slightly awkward feeling now in debt to him. What happens if another job comes along – after all how could I apply after he remarked that it was because of me being taken on by the Scottish Episcopal Church that he was now able to retire? After work I picked up a form from Joan's: having picked up a bad cold last Thursday she looked terrible with rings around her eyes: still, she was cheery. Yesterday Aunt Dottle had baked the Christmas cake and had now turned her hand to a fruit cake.

1985 Powderhall I trained at Arthurs Seat this morning doing a similar sprint session as yesterday but this time on the grass. What a difference with far less impact on my Achilles tendons – so much more gentle. If the worst comes to the worst I could rearrange my training accordingly. Also the surroundings are much more interesting - there's always something going on, a world away from the tedium of the track. At lunchtime I went out to Danderhall for the OAP Lunch Club Christmas Dinner. It was a pleasant wee affair. I collected four of them from their homes in my car and also chauffeured them home too which they all appreciated. The meal itself was passable. Some of the members sang and others danced. There were around a dozen members along plus a dozen others in attendance including the minister the Reverend Robertson, councillors (Sam Campbell), etc. At six o'clock there was a wee bit of bother at the centre from three late teenage boys. Come 6:30 p.m. it was down to Joan's for a bowl of soup. At 8:00 p.m. I helped the caretaker to put the trampolines down and away before heading back to the flat. Martha was in from Thursday late evening shopping.

1990 Colinton 7:00 p.m. Jimmy Saville is on *This Is Your Life*. Martha and Janey were in town today Christmas shopping with me just trailing behind them chauffeuring them around.

13th December

1980 Portobello It seemed to be the first steady run that I've done in ages – 4 miles and that's me half-wondering whether to enter next year's London Marathon in March! With college over for the academic term it's strange having a little bit more available leisure time with no immediate pressure that emanates from exams etc. However it's essential that I continue to keep my head down. The major goals for the Christmas Holidays are: (1) Dissertation (2) Law Assignment (3) Accounts Assignment (4) Read Econonomics Book (5) Write the Econmics Essay (6) Go through mock June Examination papers. I put an old Christmas photograph of my sister Áine and myself in to be framed at Jeffrey Street – the town was like the mad-house. I had a very lazy Saturday evening in, in front of the fire watching the box. Enoch Powel was on Parkinson – a quite fascinating man who seemed to mesmerise and captivate the audience. Outside the rain is falling and there's a fair old wind a-blowing.

PS Our Christmas Tree was brought into the house today.

1981 Portobello After Sunday lunch I sat and enjoyed Kind Hearts and Coronets before going out for a run. You get immense pleasure from looking at all the lovely decorated Christmas trees that light up many windows. Half way round the snow began to fall, softly but steadily. It drifted down, a very powdery type. I ran home via the Figgate Park where there were still one or two ghostly skaters on the ice. An evening in front of the fire whilst outside the snow continued to fall: it made Martha quite excited.

1984 Powderhall It was an unusual sort of a day for me. I took my half day which is granted to each of us for Christmas shopping.

After doing a bit I dropped into the book fair at the Assembly Rooms. If I'd had the money there were some nice buys – Dulac's Fairy Book for £15 and a book on the Pentlands that I hadn't come across before. At four o'clock I had an interview at the Traverse Theatre: it went well, however it was never on: really, they were wasting my time. With it being a Thursday I went back round the shops again. Come eight o'clock I met Martha. She took me out for a Chinese meal: it was very pleasant. Afterwards we strolled home through the capital. I enjoy being a town-dweller.

1994 Colinton This evening I think the situation on the Tristan-Isolde front looks a little less promising with Isolde intimating that it's all over between them. I'm hopeful that it's but a blip. I tried to put an optimistic front on things. From lunchtime on there was some sun, it was quite still and a cold was a-descending – a nice afternoon. At lunchtime I'd looked home afterwards taking Martha and Atticus with me back to Dalkeith with Martha buying a Christmas wreath for our front door. This evening we put up the Christmas tree and the lights: Martha's working on it as I write; meanwhile Tristan is on the phone to Isolde.

1995 Colinton A grey grey day. Joan was cheery and talkative. Just as soon as I was in the door from work Martha was straight out of the door for Thursday late night Christmas shopping meeting up with Lucille. Meanwhile Darby and I had a boys night in. I watched the film *Glitz* but mainly because I'd read the book (Elmore Leonard). It brings me pleasure to see Martha escaping on occasion knowing that she has our wee family in the hinterland to come home to.

14th December

1981 Portobello It's Monday morning and I'm sitting at my desk with a pot of coffee. Outside is the first snow of the winter – around two inches, but surprisingly the light is poor suggesting lots more snow to come. Rounding off the scene I've the Test Match on the radio coming from India – amazing, here's me in Portobello – I can also well imagine some archetypal old English colonel in the Home Counties having breakfast in his country home reading The Times with his old cabinet radio crackling away in the background.

1983 Powderhall I found work a toughish stint today, somewhat padding it out. There was a distinct change in the weather with the snow washed away and a gusty irritating wind a-blew all day long. At lunchtime I was all over the place – Jenners, the Post Office, Thin's and Bauermeister's before coming back to Grosvenor Crescent. But a mistake though because one ends up rushing around for nothing lessening the pleasure of moving slowly and enjoying the moment, but the temptation too of an hour and a half lunch hour. At tea-time I walked out to Morningside to Safeways for the Christmas tree. I walked because I felt like it. I was a bit brassed off and I enjoyed mingling with the crowds passing by to stop occasionally to look in the lit windows of the shops. There was a six-footer – perhaps a tad small, but nicely shaped. In the evening I hadn't fancied it but met up with Jonathon Butt, Dick Nossitor and Bill Murray at The Guildford Arms, a beautiful traditional old pub full of working class men. Ken Mortimer looked in. I was sorry to hear old Tom Drever had died. His son in law Bill Walker went out to Cyprus. The last time I saw Tom was last summer whilst upstairs on a bus: he was walking down toward Canonmills dressed in blue shorts and shirt. He was always very decent to me. He was a survivor. At times he could be a little myopic and rigid in his views and a tad old-fashioned – he was an interesting mixture. I recall having a meal with him in London with others the evening before I ran so well against East Germany. When I was young he used to sometimes give me lifts back to Duddingston, but never to the door – only to his bungalow at Duddingston Road and I had to walk the remaining half mile back to Durham Road.

1987 Morningside 11:00 a.m. Just before dawn broke I ran through a frost covered misty Hermitage. But what made it so special was that I came across two herons on the outward run and three, yes three, on the return. Wonderful. Yesterday, Sunday, Martha and I drove out to Roseberry to get the Christmas tree. We'd chosen a lovely day to go out with a very heavy frost leaving the countryside white. All the staff there were helpful: an old country worthy farm worker carrying the trees to people's cars. We were able to squeeze a tree in for Joan. It's such a very lovely drive through the Carrington countryside. From there we drove to Musselburgh to get the loan of a spare set of lights from Nell. Back at our Plewlands Morningside flat we set the tree up in the bay window. It looks very nice indeed. We'd spent the Saturday evening in by the fire with Martha busy wrapping presents. Twasn't like her but she reflected how lucky she was to have her mum, Janey, for Christmas and how she feels she's looking forward to Christmas and is currently making decorations. Earlier that afternoon we'd looked out to Stobsmills House with Joan and Aunt Dottle to see Margaret. It was a pleasant afternoon. The lovely Georgian house unfortunately needs a great deal of attention. It would be lovely to see what she could achieve with a couple of hundred thousand pounds. She'd made me a lovely Christmas wreath for my door, all from the grounds of her estate. I insisted on giving her £5 for it. It's now hanging on my front door and looks very classy against the black and gold. It was very cold out there in Gorebridge with the lawn covered in a white frost which didn't lift all day. She lit the open fire. On Friday past I had lunch with Dad and Fraser Henderson (Assistant Director Education Edinburgh City Council). I learnt a useful lesson. Having half-jokingly mentioned to the Midlothian District Council Chief Executive that perhaps after the booklet fiasco I should be looking for a new career I'd considered going into teaching. Dad arranged for me to meet Fraser. But when I said this to him he said he was only looking for people who wanted to teach rather than going into the profession for negative reasons. OUCH! I wont make that mistake again!

1989 Morningside There's three inches of snow on the ground. It was somewhat hazardous heading out to Midlothian for work. Are we paying for the past few easy winters? Earlier I was out running through the Hermitage but I was unable to truly appreciate it for the flecks of snow stinging my eyes. The traffic jam began just past Hillend Ski Slope. It would appear I'm the only senior member of staff who's managed to get into work. On Sunday past we went out to Roseberry this time getting a twelve footer. Martha's nephew Hoch was down from Perthshire staying with us, down for the Scotland v Romania match: we had to bundle him in the back of the car with the tree! The staff out at Roseberry are so very friendly including an old cloth-capped chap from the nursery and a younger lad of my own age doing the trees. Whilst we were arguing in fun about the size of the tree eagle-eyed Martha spotted the jump from ten feet to eleven and a half first.

15th December

1972 Portobello The bad news is that after being off a couple of weeks ago then back for four days meant that I only got £2 for my wages this week. Given I'm giving Joan £3 for my keep that makes life challenging. It was the Thomas Graham & Son Ltd. Christmas party so Roy let me get away early so that I could get myself all ready. It was held out at the Glenburn Hotel at Blinkbonny Currie and Darby gave me a lift out from Porty. It was a good evening and I was stoned. The dinner was really good too - a lot of laughs, a few dances and then Willie Fergie from the kitchen design department gave me a lift back to Portobello which was really very good of him.

1982 Portobello I bought a copy of *The Diary Of Adrian Mole Age 13 and ¾* for Martha's brother Douglas and ended up sitting reading it myself in front of the fire all afternoon whilst eating shortbread. I met Martha outside Crawford's Restaurant at the West End at 6:30 p.m. Martha, poor thing was famished – I only had coffee. We walked up a wet windy and raw Lothian Road for the Hospital Carol Service: I thought it so-so but felt the audience could have done with singing a bit more.

1984 Powderhall Martha and I went our separate ways to make a dent in our Christmas shopping. I ended up being quite successful. At Stockbridge I treated myself to my present from Áine – *Grimm's Household Tales* illustrated by Mervyn Peake for £6. In return I've bought her a shirt. I travelled from Stockbridge up to the American's bookshop at Marchmont picking up some Bookclub editions for Spieler and for John. From there I crossed town to South Clerk Street to Mackenzie's Sports Shop for Young Paul's present. Paul Forbes was there working. I spoke to him for ten minutes – he's back training again. Good to hear. Whilst I went to Stockbridge Martha went to Willie Low's. Paul D. (Dickson) came with me and we picked up the Christmas tree. It's an eight footer. Paul and Martha spent much of the evening setting it up and decorating it. It was lovely watching them work in tandem and harmony – another little positive thing in his life and development. Later on I called Joan.

1986 Powderhall Yesterday Martha and I collected the car from George Street then drove down to Glentress Forest at Innerleithen to search out a Christmas tree. Twas just like old times with the two of us together again. But no joy – the trees were poor. We drove back via Roseberry estate – very fortuitous as the trees were lovely – thick, well-shaped and tall. And the staff were very pleasant. With it being the back of two o'clock we pulled into the Cockatoo Inn at Millerhill for a Sunday pub lunch – filling, if nothing else. We enjoyed putting the tree up with The Snowman LP on in the background.

1987 Morningside 3:30 p.m. It's afternoon now and a cold winter's day. There's a white frost all around which hasn't lifted all day. I saw a single heron this morning. At lunchtime I stopped off at Joan's for a bowl of soup: she was quite chirpy, busy making more Christmas sweets, two of which I'm eating just now (fudge/marzipan) with a cup of tea. I looked into Letts at Dalkeith looking for a new diary, but no joy. I took the Whitecraigs road back to work feeling somewhat brassed off after a sarcastic phone call from the Director, John Gilfillan: en-route I was stopped by police undertaking stop checks including wanting to search my – and other drivers' – boots too! This morning I saw only one of the herons in at the Hermitage as it went flying by. Yesterday I was able to collect Martha from outside her work at five o'clock – it was lovely for us to be in from work early.

1988 Morningside It was the pensioners' Christmas lunch at Danderhall Leisure Centre today. It was very pleasant. I had to drive the poor minister, the Reverend Robertson, back home down to the manse as he felt hot and dizzy. The groundsman thought he'd had too much to drink. I've moved the settee to face onto the fire giving me a greater appreciation of it. I think the innovation came about from writing about New Year parties in days gone by at Henderson Row. I'd reflected on an enduring pleasure from years before sitting there feeling warm, secure and comfortable sitting by the box all those years ago.

1990 Colinton 10:00 a.m. Over the past few days I've been spending money in town like it's been going out of fashion. It's creating a certain dissonance. On the Thursday evening June stayed overnight – along with Martha they'd been at the WM Company Christmas night out. I've completed Fairbairn's autobiography *A Life Is Too Short* – excellent. Last evening Martha and I put up our first West Mill Christmas tree. The cats are interested! Yohanan and Lee arrived back from Portugal today.

1995 Colinton A lovely last Friday at work before escaping for the Christmas holidays rounded off appropriately with a Christmas lunch out at The Stair Arms near Pathhead: twas the usual stilted affair that happens everywhere up and down the land. As per I began the holiday with a haircut at Morningside: unbelievably I bumped into the Director-Designate: twas a stilted conversation – my star is not in the ascendancy which is disappointing and rankles.

16th December

1982 Portobello Joan and Aunt Dottle are out at the Edinburgh Sketching Club's Christmas party. It was such a foul evening it would be nice if I had a car to pick Joan up and transport her door to door – perhaps one day if I manage to secure a good job. She was very busy today – the doctor in the morning before rattling off at least three dozen orange iced buns for their evening do not to mention putting some chocolate on to the home-made peppermint creams she's made for our Christmas. After a hot bath I've sat in front of a very warm coal fire all evening reading James Drawbell's *'Scotland – Bitter Sweet'*.

1983 Powderhall I felt on a high today. It was of course Friday – my third one since starting work at the Scottish Episcopal Church and I had taken the half day they give to all staff for Christmas shopping. As for the morning there was no real work to speak of. Come mid-day I escaped into the crowds. The streets were packed with people. But I enjoyed myself, out and about buying presents for everybody – good fun. There I was battling in and then out of the Princes Street shops before heading across to George Street. There was some light rain. I bought a decanter for Áine and Spieler; several books for Mum, John and Aunt Dottle and also serendipities for Martha's Christmas stocking. Oh, and a birthday present for her too. In a very happy mood I took all my purchases back to the flat before thereafter leaving to head out to Oxgangs. At Canonmills a tramp asked me for some monies. Normally I always do but for some reason on this occasion I didn't. But instead I gave him the 3 chocolate flapjacks I was taking out for the Oxgangs crowd. So instead of hopping on a 27 bus I walked up to Hendersons at Hanover Street to buy some more to replace them before travelling out to Oxgangs for tea. In the evening I joined Lee and his mates out on the town. Four pints made me feel more than rough. But socially an interesting evening. Walking back to the flat I grabbed some pie and chips. Shortly afterwards a happily tipsy Martha arrived home from a very good Wood-Mackenzie Christmas party at the North British Hotel.

1984 Powderhall There was a heavy frost this morning. We were all surprised given it's been so mild recently. After visiting the launderette I popped down to Joan's ending up having Sunday lunch there. Joan was quite voluble about this and that. We enjoyed watching Jimmy Boyle on television alongside Cecil Parkinson and David Dimbleby. I've been reading one of the books I've bought for John's Christmas - Jeffrey Archer's *Not A Penny More Not A Penny Less* - and was rather taken with it! I spent the afternoon with Lee. He was quite chirpy - Ann's doing I'd guess. I had tea at Mum's. Áine and Spieler were along with Áine going on to him as per - and a little bit vice-versa! Torville & Dean won the BBC Sports Personality of the Year. I was home by eleven o'clock thanks to Spieler. Martha was still up: Lucille had been round wrapping Christmas presents.

1990 Colinton 4:45 p.m. It's a damp misty sort of a day, but mild, allowing me to work in the garden. I've built another step and because of the prohibitive cost I've had a re-think on the path. Caomhog, Lulu and Mum were dumped here at lunchtime to give Áine and Spieler some freedom. They enjoyed themselves. Later on we all went for a walk gathering in some holly.

1991 Colinton 9:30 a.m. Martha and I are heading off to collect our Christmas tree this morn. She was out late last evening at the Minto Hotel for her section seasonal night out. The evening before we got back from babysitting in Perth for Robbie and Helen at 3:00 a.m. in the morning! Yesterday (Saturday) I was down at Peebles with Joan and Aunt Dottle. It was very pleasant although I thought Joan was slightly out of sorts.

1992 Colinton 5:30 p.m. I was on the phone to Paul - he was quite chirpy. He's up to his neck in Christmas. I was at Joan's for lunch - she's still going on about Charles and Di. Martha and I were round at Virginia's at Learmonth Terrace last evening along with Nell for mince pies and cream and mulled wine.

17th December

1973 Portobello A very long and boring day at work at Graham's. The Prime Minister Edward Heath announced the Three Day Week Order to help conserve stocks of coal. It comes into being on Hogmanay. Meanwhile we've been told we will have to continue working, cold or not, or we'll only be paid for three days. On a happier note Joan had phoned Angus who passed on the message to me that Darby is working this afternoon so I was able to get a lift back home to Portobello and be in for dinner at a luxurious 5.30 p.m.

1978 Portobello After lunch the temperature plummeted - zeroed! It was freezing. Darby (my grandfather) dropped me off out at Oxgangs however, I didn't quite run all the way back. As I came along Church Lane in Duddingston Village I was surprised to come across Darby chatting to a policeman. Evidently a woman had pranged his car. We desperately need to get it paid out of her insurance.

1993 Colinton I began the day with a good session out at Danderhall Leisure Centre followed by a couple of cheese toasties for breakfast. I headed into town and managed to buy a few Christmas presents. I was out all day. As per last year I parked the car at the Holyrood Park Car Park and simply walked up The Royal Mile, down to Princes Street before returning via The Grassmarket and Chambers Street. All in all a successful time.

18th December

1972 Oxgangs *Get A New Diary - Got It OK* A new week at Thomas Graham but once again it was fine. When you've had a great weekend you forget all about it and then it's good to get back into a groove again. People were talking away about the Christmas party at the Glenburn Hotel. Everyone seems to have enjoyed themselves and there were a few sore heads. Anyway it made for quite a good atmosphere around Balcarres Street today.

1974 Portobello I had a long lie in bed this morning. In the afternoon Darby and I went out to the Edinburgh Fruit Market to look for a Christmas tree, however we were out of luck. After being out at Oxgangs Lucy told Darby that she would get him one. In the evening we reckon Paul can get back off with Lorraine Morris. I managed to write out some Christmas cards.

1979 Portobello After a coffee and collecting the milk from the top of Durham Road I went out for a run. Boy was it cold and I was tired. At lunchtime I had another game of squash with Bill. In the afternoon I wrapped up Sally's Christmas present and was just about to start some Accounts when I fell asleep. Come the evening I ran my best session up at Meadowbank for a while with Ken (Glass) and Paul. I'm in bed now reading the Festive Season TV guides - the Radio Times and the TV Times.

1982 Portobello Despite this damned infection I awoke early so went out for an hour's run. These colds etc. continue to bug me as they've done now for a decade. It was a frosty crisp morn and I'd only really intended running to the village and back but for whatever reason I diverted into the Queen's Park and up the steps adjacent to Duddingston Loch. After toiling to the top I went round by Dunsapie Loch and floated down taking another diversion, this time by Craigentinny Golf Course and back home – with a bit of a temperature! I spent the morning pottering around. Martha did some Christmas cards and wrapped some presents too. On the way to Safeways we stopped by the gate to speak to The Brashes – a nice wee chinwag with Jimmy inviting me along to his evening golf classes at Moray House in the new year – excellent. Martha got her hair done whilst I remained home. Later on we met in Portobello to pick up the Christmas tree. Joan wasn't pleased with the size of it feeling it's too small. Most unfortunate. It was the last episode of *Shogun* which I found unsatisfactory whilst Martha enjoyed the programme about Kingswood School this time featuring the pupils' A Level results – poor things. I though Martha was a bit tired and distant this evening so I nipped out to surprise her with a bag of Cadbury's Roses.

1983 Powderhall Today was a superb Saturday, from early morning until late-late in the day - a really happy and contented Saturday perhaps all enhanced with this being the third weekend since I commenced work, thus making me enjoy and savour the weekend all the more. I've changed my exercise programme and did some speed-work along a quiet stretch of the Water of Leith I stopped off at Taylor's Bakery at Canonmills to pick up a couple of bran loaves and headed back for breakfast. Martha and I walked up to town with Nell and Richard before heading off in our separate directions. We picked up Christmas presents for Nell, Roddy, Yohanan and Z. bumping into Mum at John Lewis's. The town was busier than I can ever recall it. After our a-wanderings we caught a bus at Charlotte Square back to the flat – we were laden down with six bagfuls. Home to toasted cheese before Martha wrapped Roddy's present. Young Paul from downstairs chummed me out to Meggetland – Dad was glad to see me and I was glad to see him too. Even although twas in the opposite direction he ended up giving me a lift back to Dunedin Street and stopped by for a cuppa. He was telling us he's heading out to Australia in February for a court case and may take both Bette and Roddy with him. I'm unsure how advisable that would be - he doesn't look that well to me. But I enjoyed seing him again and after he left I felt a certain emptiness inside. I really should try to see him far more often. In the evening it was a joy to sit in our 'Christmas room' - twas warm and cosy. I sat and wrote out a Santa letter to Kirk and Kent. Yohanan telephoned twice and is coming down to visit us tomorrow. Lee telephoned too - he was chirpy despite a hangover from the Friday evening before but had still managed to give his phone number to a lady of the night. Young Paul was up with us until late in the evening.

1987 Morningside 10:30 a.m. I'm a bit stressed just now and I feel it's showing in various ways. I was very ratty with both the kids at the football yesterday and also with Martha. I was surprised to hear from Yohanan on the telephone saying that both Mother and he feel I should put on Christmas this year. It raised my spirits - I'm very much looking forward to rising to the challenge. On this morning's run the weather was very mild.

1993 Colinton Martha was at the hairdresser's for nine o'clock so Joan and Aunt Dottie had to be on their marks by 9:30 a.m. I telephoned Jenners to pass on a message to Martha to say I'd pick her up and the four of us headed out to the Scottish Modern Art Gallery for morning coffee before thereafter visiting the Calton Gallery to see their Christmas Exhibition. Joan almost persuaded me to buy an Alan Sutherland for £400. She was amusingly eccentric to the gallery owner - 'Alan Sutherland was ditched by a girl' - 'I paint from nature.' - 'As for modern art!' Martha gave her £50 toward the bedspread which Joan had given her as a present. In the afternoon we travelled out to Carrington picking up a couple of neps, however Roseberry Estate is not selling Christmas trees this year so Martha and I got a Noble Spruce instead at Newington former railway station way - eight feet tall for £32. An evening in.

1995 Colinton I wasn't 100% this Sunday - somewhat light-headed. Atticus and I made slow progress back from Colinton Village: he gives lovely greetings to each and every passerby which cheers them up along their journey. At twenty months he is of course at a delightful age. We were round at M. and Virginia's in the afternoon along with Dave from Temple and children and Viv, Mourat and Yasmin. As ever M. was ungracious driving Martha bananas although I feel he is less aggressive toward me. The chap Dave meanwhile was wrapped up in his own intellect, but cruising, doing what had to be done socially. I found it all somewhat easier than Martha. We've been invited to Viv and Mourat's for dinner next January.

18th December 1995 Colinton I cleared the library. Martha took Atticus to see Santa Claus – he created somewhat, although outside mainly as he didn't wish to go in!

19th December

1971 Oxgangs *Note To Self - Boroughmuir Christmas Dance* Apart from nipping out to Colinton Mains to get the Sunday rolls and papers I stayed inside at 6/2 all day - not like me at all but I fair enjoyed myself. We gave Mum a big hand to put up the decorations for Christmas - they look pretty good. They totally transform the living room. The countdown's begun with no Boroughmuir and the prospect of us all having the family and friends about the place is really exciting and something to look forward to with great anticipation. I've definitely got that wee seasonal glow. It's also the first time the old boy isn't a part of it all. I spoke too soon about the good weather yesterday as it was very windy all day and the rain is absolutely pouring down. Again that's part of the reason why it was good to be inside and cosy with all the family today. After we put up the decorations and had dinner we settled back to watch David Copperfield with W.C. Fields brilliant as *Mr Micawber*. I just love Dickens and any of his films always gets you in the mood for the mid-winter festivals. At teatime there was Carols for Christmas on too all nicely starting the build up to the big day. I've just finished watching the telly; I'm now through in my bedroom and about to do some reading.

1974 Portobello I started my student holiday job working for the Royal Mail at the end of London Road on the Christmas post. Well that was a big mistake. In the week afterwards I ended up spending much of my pay at the physio getting my shoulder massaged and sorted out. Wimp.

1979 Portobello First thing I ran 5 miles: it was pretty cold. Come lunchtime I met Ken Glass and was running fairly well only losing contact with him on the last 50 metres of each of the four 300s. Mum and John were both down in the afternoon. I managed to do a little bit of Accounts before a large dinner and supper. I was feeling pretty tired. In the evening I relaxed watching Speed King – all about Sir Malcolm Campbell's obsession is to win the World's Land Speed Record in his car Bluebird. I'm feeling pretty low these past few days. There was a 'The Dumps' card in the post this morning from Sally. She hadn't hung around it penning it on her arrival home to the North West Coast from Edinburgh evening. She wrote:

Dear Samuel

Perhaps I found the right card! I am sitting in the sitting-room having just been to the pub which is, conveniently, next door, with Dick (step-father). I am not literally feeling as the card suggests but if I let myself think about it too long I may be. Oh dear stop being sentimental, I am longing (looking – Freudian Slip!) forward to seing you soon – that's more positive, eh, Peter?). Tomorrow is another day and I haven't decided what to do tomorrow, perhaps I'll organise things which Mother wants done before Xmas!

We will see!

Thinking of you and loving you.

Sally x

I'm down in the dumps without you (card message)

Merry Christmas

Whee A.

1989 Morningside 2:00 p.m. It's been a frosty and bright sort of a day (Tuesday), my second last at work before breaking up for a seasonal fortnight's winter break. At lunchtime I looked into the bank taking out a fiver from a recently discovered old bank book. It also turned out there were years of interest which had accumulated giving me an extra £8 so I was able to give Joan a tenner to help her along. She was saying to me how worried she gets when she thinks about Aunt Dottle's future situation. I said perhaps AUNT DOTTLE should investigate what the house might be sold to her for and whether it might be possible for us to purchase it jointly. I was up in the attic taking out the Lego for Hoch: whilst up there I came across a large old bag chockful of old tracksuits which might do some of the kids. I intend to stick them into the launderette on the way home. Last night we had June (from

Martha's work) staying over whilst on Saturday evening we had Roddy who stayed on after he had come through to Edinburgh to deliver the Christmas presents earlier in the afternoon. The weather had been atrocious with heavy rain coming on top of the snow meaning we were inches deep in slush. On the Saturday evening we went to see *Venus Peter* along with Lucille and Virginia before coming back to the flat for mince pies and cream.

20th December

1977 Portobello Joan and I picked up Darby from the hospital. I used the stairs to come down; however they ended up getting stuck in the lift for 10 minutes - just as well it wasn't an emergency! I find that at this time of the year 11.00 a.m. in the morning is the best part of a winter's day. The sun always seems to catch Arthurs Seat and it was bathed in a lovely soft warm glow. I played squash for an hour with Coach Walker; it was too long and I lost a bit interest as it wasn't very competitive. We sat in the front room by the light of the Christmas tree playing bagatelle - always good fun. The tree is lovely and Aunt Dottle bought replacement bulbs. In the evening I ran a good session with John Scott - he was running well. Along with Paul the three of us are running the half mile at the AAA Indoor Championships next month at Cosford - my first serious attempt at the distance. A mist descended so quickly and was so thick that we couldn't see parts of the track which made it interesting for running in - a real peasouper; I wouldn't have been surprised to see Sherlock Holmes emerge from the gloom. I hate to imagine how Arthurs Seat looked; you would have been stumbling around in the dark. I'm now lying in bed with the Christmas version of the Radio Times. To borrow from John Masefield's The Box of Delights and more appropriately on this foggy evening - When The Wolves Were Running...

1978 Portobello It was a stunningly beautiful winter's morning – really quite beautiful with a very heavy white frost which had coated and engulfed everything – Jack Frost's magic fingers. It was very fresh out. Sitting in the front room with our Christmas tree lit up and the cat nestling by the bay window looking out was a lovely wee moment – the simple pleasures in life. I worked on Accounts again until eleven o'clock when I went up to Arthurs Seat to run a very good session of hill runs. Darby picked me up from there at one o'clock. Mum was down so it was good to see her. I worked all afternoon before travelling out after tea to Oxgangs. And from there come seven o'clock in the evening I ran the 7 miles back down to Porty. It was quite wonderful making my way down through the Braids, Cluny and Blackford looking at all the lit-up Christmas trees in the bay windows of the fine old stone-built houses. I ran over a fair old snowfall. However by the time I got to t'other side of Arthurs Seat a thaw had begun, the temperature rose and it began to rain - at four o'clock it was minus one and now here it was four degrees centigrade. I'm sitting down now to continue reading *A Christmas Carol*. I'm feeling tired physically but I'm very much looking forward to being on holiday for the next couple of weeks over Christmas and New Year.

1979 Portobello I stayed in all morning waiting for Paul to ring but the beggar never did. - most annoying being tied to the house. Considering how very cold it was I put in another good session running a couple of 600s on my own in 81 seconds before a hill session at Arthurs Seat. Come six o'clock I ran six miles. In the evening Joan, Aunt Dottle and I all trundled up to Safeways - with Christmas a-coming they've got lots of delicious items in stock. And so to bed - early.

1980 Portobello It was a wet damp Saturday morning. Whilst I did an early morning hill session the snow stung my eyes. It was a steady tumble of snow. I looked into Mum's for an hour - really just to hand in Áine and Yohanan's Christmas cheques from Dad. I travelled down to 6 Henderson Row to hand in the Christmas cards to Margaret (Ross). It was rather lovely to be on the end of an invitation to dinner on Boxing Day.

1981 Portobello A high wind in Portobello, but last evening has brought on a great thaw. The hard packed snow and ice of the past week is rapidly disappearing. Martha and I had walked down in the sleet to get a Christmas tree, but bad news - there were none! In the evening we met her friend for a Sunday evening meal at Rock Bottom - an American-style eatery. We enjoyed tucking in handsomely - I had the chilli-con carne whilst they settled for the hamburgers all followed by a wonderful desert of cream, ice cream, banana, hot fudge, etc. known as an Elmer! The (34th) Salvation Army City Carol Service at the Usher Hall began at 8:30 p.m. I thought it not bad, but a bit long-winded in places and perhaps too many performances by those on stage and not enough mass participation. However, I enjoyed the whole evening as did we all.

1990 Colinton I'm on holiday. Tuesday was my last day. I'm off for a glorious two weeks. I'm looking forward to it but I'm only too aware it will fly by. I was keen to take time off before the official festive break rather than like some colleagues who are doing it t'other way around. Yesterday afternoon I played golf – it was very cold indeed –Lee and Yohanan beat Ray and me, but it was a close match. Given my consistency I would have ended up with the best score of all. In the morn I had a close-cut haircut.

1991 Colinton There was an inch or two of snow in Colinton this morning with half a dozen cars stuck at the top of the road (West Mill Road) – black ice. Twas highly illegal but I did some lateral thinking and took both Martha's Ford Fiesta and the Volvo 240 Estate along the Water of Leith emerging at Spylaw Street with Martha all of a tremor! I was on the phone to my sister – she wants a Transvision Vamp video for Christmas!

1994 Colinton Martha and I went out to the Gyle – we spent £146 in Safeways alone with Martha footing the bill. We were in the shop for so long I ended up reading both *The Times* and *The Scotsman*.

1995 Colinton It was very very cold this morning: mid-morning the hut at the foot of the garden was reading minus seven degrees. Joan telephoned at lunchtime to say Aunt Dottle had a half day which was good ending our dithering around. I drove down to pick them up taking the scenic route back to Colinton via Pencaitland, Temple, Cauldwell Moor and Auchendinny through a wintry landscape spoilt only by the low sun in the west shining directly into our faces. Whilst Martha went to the dentist for a filling we had afternoon tea. They stayed on for dinner: I ferried Aunt Dottle to her class allowing Joan to spend the evening in company. As I looked upon her presence I thought of all the love and the pleasure she has given me over the years and appreciated the immensity of it all having her in our wee cottage this evening. We talked about Darby and days back in the mid-1950s when I was (son) Atticus's age now and the pleasure it gave him to have me about the house at that time and of how they had bought me a (Hornby) train set and a rocking horse which the old boy had turfed out. When driving Joan home down The Mound to collect Aunt Dottle I could hardly believe this car swing illegally to the right on to Princes Street and we ran straight into him. It would seem there wasn't too much damage. The guy was genuinely sorry not wishing to have the police involved – he's a mature student. I acquiesced. He's going to call round tomorrow. Eighty-seven year old Joan was only a little shaken. (Afterwards some shock kicked in and she needed to be given either a brandy or sherry by Aunt Dottle.)

The Winter Solstice – 21st December

1971 Oxgangs We're on the countdown to Christmas. I did my papers first thing. School's still in but not for me or Paul either. He was off skiving too but at this time of the year it could hardly be described as skiving in the true sense of the word. The two of us ended up playing for much of the day both outside and inside too. Meanwhile Mum and John are on holiday and the two of them were off in to town for much of the day; they said Princes Street was pretty busy. In the evening I watched a wee bit of telly but it was surprisingly poor for this time of the year - the film *Dangerous Exile* was just historical hokum. I ended up talking with Mum and John for quite a while.

1972 Oxgangs After work I went training but it was a real beggar as not only did I forget my spikes but also my training shoes too; a bit of a disaster although I managed to do something. Anne Johnstone was looking great; I think I'll send her a Christmas card. Before going home a few of us got a good wee game of basketball going - quite enjoyable. Paul and I quite like practising our penalty shots. I've got my own technique which is pretty accurate including the ability to launch the ball from a long way out. Later on I went home to watch *Colditz*. It was good as usual – *Tweeddledum* - all about an officer feigning madness to escape. However the ending was unsettling; whilst he returns to England a letter arrives from his wife to say he really does end up being mad and there's little hope for him.

1973 Portobello Oh well back to the 'hole' (working as a Junior Cost Clerk at Thomas Graham & Sons Ltd. Builders & Plumbers Merchants 51 Balcarres Street Morningside). It was real bad having to sit and do the lines all day. On top of that Roy (my boss) was taking the crap out of me. At lunchtime I popped along to Morningside and had a hamburger supper. Willie Fergie and I went to the Cash 'n Carry in his wee Hillman Imp. I bought three boxes of liqueurs as fancy wee Christmas presents; they look pretty good and I'm pleased with them. When I walked along Balcarres

Street after work wee Áine (sister) was already in the car at Cluny Avenue. She's staying tonight. I gave Bill (Walker athletics coach) a ring in the evening to ask permission to train with Stewart McCallum who I'd bumped into at Meadowbank.

1974 Portobello There was a very colourful postcard in the post this morning from Bjorg Larsen in Oslo. She'd sent a Christmas postcard of a cheery but slightly sinister looking goblin figure with a long white straggly beard carrying a staff with a sack of presents on his back and a lit up lodge in the background; snow is falling on snow, deep. *'To Samuel. I wish you a Merry Christmas and a Happy New Year' Love from Bjorg*

1975 Portobello I looked in to Meadowbank at mid-day. A. gave me a card and a medallion for Christmas. Norman Gregor dropped me off at home after training and I relaxed in watching John Wayne in *The Alamo*. I drove out to Oxgangs. Mum kindly gave me my bus pass monies. I stayed on until seven before coming home. As per usual Captain Poldark was enjoyable as was *Anne of the Thousand Days*.

1976 Portobello Bjorg sent her annual colourful card from Oslo: 'Hi Samuel, These are just a few words for Christmas to you. I'm feeling well and train a lot, but not so much as in earlier years. I have too much to do with my job. My work in a hospital with old people is very interesting but very hard. I am often free in the middle of the day and then work to 7 or 8 pm. I have not tried skiing yet but there's a lot of snow here now and very cold I think. I will start in a new job in January and then I will get regular working time and can train more than I do now. I hope you're getting on well in your training and wish you good luck for next season. I wish you Merry Christmas and a Happy New Year. Lots of love from Bjorg.' Given it's the winter solstice and as we move towards the mid-winter festivals and the end of the year, a wet but relatively mild day for this time of the season. On the way back from work at the Scottish Council of Social Service Claremont Crescent the Triumph Spitfire was giving me a little bit bother and I ended up putting the battery on a charge overnight

1977 Portobello We took Joan along to Safeways to get in the Christmas messages. They came to over £18. I picked up a couple of cases of Babycham to have in handy in my bedroom for a future occasion. After lunch Darby and I drove out to Marchmont Road to see my brother Yohanan about the turkey. Both he and Z. looked awful, like death warmed up and very white. I'm to collect the bird tomorrow. It's surprising because according to the girl at Davidson-Scott Butchers he left the business a week ago. They gave me a small present. It's quite exciting feeling the parcel. I've placed it under our Christmas tree. We dropped by Oxgangs to visit Mum. I wish she wouldn't go on about Dad in front of my girlfriend - talk about washing your dirty linen in public. I put in a good training session and sat in for the evening at home by a glowing coal fire.

1978 Portobello I'm feeling very tired mentally and physically, noticing it on the run up to Meadowbank, but pushed through running an excellent track session. I slept all afternoon before going to Safeways to get in the last messages before Christmas. I ran a good session with Ross Nicol. Paul Forbes was steamboats. I went across to The Golden Gates afterwards joining Paul in a tipple. I had a pint. We finished off the evening with a baked potato.

1980 Portobello It was a bit cold and damp. I only managed a couple of hours of Accounts today and then sat around reading the Sunday newspapers. I went alone to a lovely Christmas Carol service at Charlotte Chapel myself this evening. I enjoy singing carols. Home for a large supper.

1981 Portobello Last evening Martha and I quite enjoyed the City Carol Service at the Usher Hall with her friend Shirley. Today's the shortest day of day-light. And early on it lived up to that, very dark out. I ran four miles along Portobello Promenade; it was still icy in parts but I ran at a good pace. I dropped by Martha's flat at Gayfield Square but the door was locked. I spent an hour up town and tried again - success! We struggled back to Porty with a couple of bagfuls. A happy relaxed evening in. Paul phoned in the morning. It doesn't look it, but it was actually a very busy day what with letter writing etc.

1982 Portobello Courtesy of Wood-Mackenzie, Martha had the day off to enjoy some Christmas shopping. I meanwhile ran four miles and along with Joan went for the messages before joining Martha for lunch at Jenners' Rose Street Restaurant. I liked my baked potato but Martha thought her pizza was slightly undercooked. We spent a very pleasant few hours in the Edinburgh Bookshop and Menzies before returning to Jenners for afternoon tea - a chocolate éclair. I dashed about looking for a lady who had left a lovely scarf – Martha eventually found her. Home. Tea. And a relaxed evening in. I feel life is just rushing by, but happily so.

1983 Powderhall How odd – I went all day thinking it was Tuesday (it was Wednesday!). I worked solidly at the Episcopal all the day long mainly on a trial balance – not an unenjoyable way to spend work as I became quite absorbed in the work. Jackie was irritable all morning and then in contrast a too much to drink ebullient mood in the afternoon – quite a contrast. I was the main focus of both barrels, the morning and the afternoon, the drawback of sharing an office with her. Actually, now that I think about that, it was yesterday. Anyway, come five o'clock I was off on my bike to cycle back home to the flat. En-route I thought that's me on the exercise front for the day treating myself to a pie supper on the journey. As Martha was out for an office Christmas meal I spent the evening out at Oxgangs at Lee's. I'm glad I did; his father was there and we had some excellent belly laughs. I also enjoyed a good chat with him on the theme of Christmas. He thought it a time for hypocrites. I said I was too much of a romantic enjoying the festival season to mount any sensible counter-argument seeing it through rose-tinted spectacles. He went on to say that people were hypocrites all the year round with Christmas showing them up and he couldn't really blame Christmas for being themselves. Later on Julie came in. She was cheery, especially so as both Lee's have agreed to join her at the daughter in law's (Ricky's wife) for the big day. She kindly rattled up some egg toast for us all. We watched a thriller – *The Fog* – entertaining hokum. It finished quite late on, so much so I was risking missing the last bus – fortunately a quick sprint saw me catch it across town. I lay in bed reading Graham Swift's *Waterland* with a Leonard Rossiter short film on in the background. A rather merry Martha arrived home at 1:30 a.m. waking me up just as I was drifting off to sleep – I'm glad to say.

1984 Powderhall I've sent a Father Christmas letter to my nephews, Kirk and Kent at 4/5 Hailesland Gardens Edinburgh:

Dear Kirk and Kent,

Hello there men - Santa here.

I just wanted to write to say a big thank you for all your help.

Oh!, hold on a minute, that's one of the dwarves shouting at me - I think it's Wee Jocky the Scottish dwarf.

'Santa, dinnae be silly man, Kirk and Kent will no remember.'

'And why not?' asked Santa.

'Why not!' exclaimed Jocky 'because it wiz all done wie magic - that's why not! And even if they did remember, they'd jist think it wiz all a dream.'

'Oh, I see' said Santa with a sad look, 'that is a shame. Now I won't be able to write a thank you letter to these two brave Scots laddies.'

Wee Jocky felt sorry for Santa. He knew how much Santa wanted to thank Kirk and Kent for all their help in finding the stolen Christmas toys - if not for them, there would have been no Christmas, 1984 for children all over the world.

Jocky turned to Santa and said 'although it's against the rules, I suppose you could break it this once to write to them about it all and to thank them.'

Santa's face immediately brightened up. 'Right Jocky, where will I begin?'

'At the beginning of course Santa. Tell them how Troublesome Tommy (aka T.T.) and the Goblins sneaked into the toy factory and stole all the toys.'

So, Santa took up the sad story.

Two days before Christmas, the dwarves and I had just finished all the year's work. We had just made the very last two toys. Funny enough they were for you two boys, Kirk and Kent.

Well, we were knackered and dead beat. I was the last out the factory. But, I was so tired I forgot to lock the factory gates. And that night T.T. the rebellious dwarf (remember boys how he led last year's strike?) and twenty of the nastiest, ugliest and smelliest goblins that you ever saw-or smelt, crept in to the factory during the night and stole every single toy.

Well, the dwarves and I didn't hear a thing. The tiredness meant we slept soundly; Mrs Claus said you could hear me snoring in Wester Hailes, Edinburgh!

But, the reindeers had heard them-in fact they'd smelt them, but unfortunately were all tied up. Rudolf tried to warn me, 'Santa! Santa!' he shouted 'Please wake up - we're being robbed.' But unfortunately I just continued to snore; Mrs Claus says I could snore for Scotland!

And also one of the goblins kicked poor Rudolf right up the hooter!

Shut up!' he screamed ''or I'll shut you up for good!'' now reindeers are gentle creatures, so on hearing these threats they all immediately lay down and covered their eyes with their hooves.

The following morning, Christmas Eve, just imagine our horror? An empty factory!'

'What will we do?' we all wailed.

Well, it was obvious, we needed someone clever to track the robbers down.

'How about Kirk Pepys?' shouted Jocky 'He's supposed to be a right wee clever clogs.'

I said 'That's a brilliant idea Jocky - well done.' But added, 'We could also do with someone who's handy in a fight. You know, good with a sword.'

Sleepy-Head Sammy awoke and said 'What about Kent Pepys, Kirk's brother? I hear he's very brave.'

So, that very day I sent for the Pepys boys. I sent Jocky and Sammy on my super-speed sledge, with an extra two reindeer tied to the back.

In the blink of an eye they were by your bedside at Wester Hailes. You boys were still fast asleep, so Jocky sprinkled some magic dust on you both. Kent sneezed! 'Trust him!' said Kirk. Jocky then told the boys about Santa's problem.

'Now, will you help out?' he asked.

'Of course we will' said Kent.

'Great!' said Jocky' your reindeers await-they're sitting outside the bedroom window.'

Kirk looked out the window in amazement-he could hardly believe his eyes-both reindeers were hovering in the sky.

The boys climbed and on to the reindeers' backs, then WHOOSH! They were off, flying-up and away!

Kirk got such a shock he almost fell off. Meanwhile Kent was loving it. He rode the reindeer with only one hand on the rein. 'That's good Kent' shouted Jocky 'that means you can use your other hand to wield a sword.'

After, travelling at super-speed they soon arrived back at the empty toy factory. Did you ever see a sadder sight? Santa immediately told the boys the whole story.

'Hmm' said Kirk 'very interesting'. Then he dipped in to his pocket and brought out his thinking cap and put it on his head. Immediately his brain grew to twice its size! Meanwhile Kent was practicing his sword moves with a big shiny sword that one of the dwarves had handed him.

With the thinking cap on his head, Kirk paced up and down with his fore-finger across his lips. He walked about the factory in search of clues. Every now and then he would pause and scratch his head. Santa followed Kirk up and down, back and forward, but kept at a safe distance.

He was optimistic that Kirk could solve the mystery.

Of a sudden Kirk shouted out. 'Got it!' he cried out. He had found something. It was something that had come from a nasty goblin.

'But they're only twigs' said all the dwarves in unison. 'Yes' said Kirk straightening up his thinking cap 'but think about it - there are no trees up here in the Northlands - are there?'

'No' all the dwarves shouted together 'It's far too cold!'

'Exactly' said Kirk. 'Twigs...branches...woods' we heard Kirk mutter to himself. 'How do goblins travel?' asked Kirk.

Wee Jocky piped up 'Sometimes on witches' broomsticks if the witches are on holiday.'

'So' said Kirk 'as this is the season of light and joy-the witches are on holiday; they've been banished to the dark lands. I bet you, pound to a penny, the goblins have travelled here from Witches Wood. And that's where the stolen toys will be.'

In an instant Sammy, Jocky and Kirk were on board Santa's sledge flying in the direction of Witches Wood; meanwhile Kent led a platoon of sixty dwarves riding through the dark night skies on the backs of reindeers.

Soon they arrived at the wood and spotted the goblins' camp. It was Kirk who first smelled the pong. Phew!' he said, whilst holding his nose.

Santa's small army crept very quietly up on the camp; he told everyone to be as quiet as a mouse 'And no farting either!' However, just as they encroached on the camp, poor Santa, being so plump stepped on a twig. It snapped! A goblin shouted out. Soon the camp was alive with goblins scampering up and down, shoving each other out the way as they attempted to run away and escape by squeezing down burrows. This was proving difficult as they were also trying to hide all the toys.

Santa announced he would smoke them all out.

'Oh, don't do that' said Troublesome Tommy, but slyly with a horrible grin 'Instead, let's reach a compromise.'

'What do you suggest?' said Santa.

'I suggest man to man combat to see who gets to keep the toys. The goblin champion against Santa's champion.'

'Okay' said Santa 'fair enough; now, who will we pick?' he asked

Wee Jocky, his most trusted dwarf

'Kent. He's very good with a sword.' All the other dwarves agreed.

So, Kent rode out on Rudolf Reindeer's back. In one hand he held the rein. In the other hand, his trusted sword.

The goblins' champion was horrible. And ferocious. He had a big pimple on his nose. But Kent didn't worry. Soon, he was dodging blows. The fight went on for five minutes. And then, with one mighty swipe of his blade, he cut the goblin's head off. It hit the ground, then rolled slowly all the way downhill into a river. PLOP! SPLASH! It landed in the water and could be last seen floating downstream.

'Hurrah! Hurrah!' shouted all the dwarves 'we've got the toys back.

Kirk and Kent have saved Christmas!'

'Three cheers for the two boys.' said Santa.

He put both arms around them.

Of a sudden Kirk and Kent awoke in their beds back at Hailesland Gardens. But, it was Mum with her arms around them both. 'You must have been dreaming boys.' she said.

But we know better - don't we boys?"

Happy Christmas!

Love from Santa.

1988 Morningside 8.30 p.m. I was standing at the sink in the small former scullery area thinking I'll have to cancel the arrangements for Martha's birthday party tomorrow when the most terrible catastrophe was announced in a break on the Radio Scotland Iain Anderson programme. A Jumbo en-route from London to New York has crashed over buildings; there are hundreds of casualties. It happened over Lockerbie, Dumfries. The news stunned me. I raced through to the bedroom to give Martha the shocking news where she was in bed with a bad virus, cough and streaming eyes having called off from her department's Christmas night out. In my dreams or nightmares I've had an occurring dream of such a happening over Oxgangs watching a plane getting lower and lower in the sky until it's having to try to weave in and out of buildings but I never imagined anything similar might happen in reality over Scotland.

1989 Ullapool Martha and I drove up to Ullapool from Morningside. We stopped off at Perthshire for a sandwich looking in to visit her brother Robbie who's still down with a touch of the flu. Helen was very pleasant. We enjoyed our drive up the A9 stopping off in The Northlands and Wyvis (the farm) to pick up some meat for her sister. I didn't enjoy staying at Ullapool. Her sister is too aggressive for my liking. I felt on the defence from the minute I stepped over the doorstep. I find her selfish and ungrateful. She was complaining about the gift of meat from her father and going on about her expectations of presents from others too. She'd take anything and everything from Martha. What really gets my goat is she appreciates nothing yet expects everything.

1990 Morningside Yohanan and I looked out to Livingston for lunch to see Dad. He'd been in hospital yesterday with a painful muscle spasm. He's on painkillers. He's lost a lot of weight recently. It's a bit of a worry. However he perked up when he saw the two of us. Later on back at West Mill, Yohanan and I enjoyed watching Stanley Baxter in *The Fast Lady* chuckling away – such an amusing feel-good film.

1992 Colinton (3.00 pm) I phoned Martha at the farm this morning to wish her a happy birthday. She was busy in the kitchen with Sheila (Bruce's wife over from Australia for Christmas) icing three Christmas cakes. Meanwhile Bruce was out singeing and preparing turkeys. It must be very strange for them all - this mix of a birthday; the festive season and being across here at the family home, yet all awhile with the great sadness of their mum Janey dying in hospital and the inevitability of her fragile condition hovering over them.

1993 Colinton Martha's sister and her two boys Loki and Thor arrived at West Mill from Ullapool via the Black Isle where they picked up two turkeys – one for Robbie and Helen in Perthshire and one for ourselves.

1994 Colinton I was in all morning and out all afternoon. I saw Mother at Joan's for a bowl of soup and to hand in Christmas presents for Áine and the girls. It was very cold out with the frost not lifting all day long but giving the Edinburgh streets and the countryside a magical dusting and sparkly Christmas feel to the world. I managed all my stops including buying a card from Atticus and me to give to Martha for her birthday tomorrow. Travelling from Stockbridge to Portobello. I stopped off at Broughton Books. How on earth does the guy make a living? It must be a year since I was last in his shop and I never buy anything. The TV personality, broadcaster and writer Muriel Gray was there buying something. She's shaven away her hair at the sides of her head making for an interesting look. The owner of the shop – Peter – followed by a Polish name, whilst still young in appearance is slowly growing old in the shop. He was sitting typing out a letter at a cheap typewriter circa 1970. He's an unusual character. Whilst always very courteous and polite I always find any interaction with him slightly awkward. I may be wrong but I think he's possibly homosexual. When he first bought the shop he was young and vital – now I suspect the dissonance of shop life has slowly soaked in and been absorbed into his being and his soul. There's a lot of deadwood in the stock with very little outflow or inflow of material thus lessening any desire to visit the shop more regularly. It's a vicious cycle.

Martha was out in the evening at the annual Wood-Mackenzie Christmas do; before leaving Colinton she had a twenty minute panic but eventually found her spectacles. She joined Lucille at a Christmas Carol Concert followed by dinner at the Sheraton Hotel. The food was so good she was in no hurry to come home. Atticus (aged 8 months) started greeting towards midnight.

1995 Colinton A very Christmassy view out as I sit here in the library. It began with just a light flutter of snow at the Gyle when Martha, Atticus and I were out getting in the messages. We were buying in something for Martha's birthday tomorrow and also for next Monday's Christmas lunch. I spent the afternoon on my own – a nice break to Morningside. I bought what I think is a ghastly-looking outfit for my niece Jennifer's Barbie doll. And from there did some hill repetitions on the slope adjacent to Blackford Pond. It was very still out with a light coating of white. The pond itself had a covering of ice. With dusk fast descending the local birds, ducks and swans were gathering in for the night. Essentially I had the place to myself bar one romantic couple; a triumvirate of ladies and one old chap who I passed at regular intervals. It felt hallowed ground and quite restful. On my cool-down jog I passed by warm and inviting lit windows seeing young faces inside playing happily away and of course thought of Atticus and his new sibling to be less than three months hence. Several of the bedrooms had bunk-beds in them. A haunting early evening somehow enhanced by the knowledge that I was going home to Colinton to my own little family. Earlier in the morning the chap who had caused the accident (by illegally turning right onto Princes Street at the foot of the Mound) looked by. We both felt sorry for the lad. He's not well off – after redundancy, no flat and kicking off a new career in outdoor education he's paying the bill for the damage done to our Volvo – £631. Meanwhile wee Atticus is thriving becoming demanding and independent.

1996 The Northlands Martha's sister gave Atticus and me a lift into Inverness Railway Station. Atticus was very tired and gurney at 5.30 am – it's no wonder as he didn't go to his bed until midnight. Whilst dressing him this morning and with the rest of the household still fast asleep I thought 'Samuel, this is a big mistake'. But how wrong was I. For the first hour of the journey, along with the train driver, he was the only person awake. He had an ice lolly, crisps and some milk. Thereafter he slept for the remaining two hours all the way to

Edinburgh. At that age and me creatively turning a couple of tops into pillows for him you can really become quite comfortable. I meanwhile read the paper and half-dozed. The train is excellent for getting you right into the heart of Edinburgh city centre. We dumped a couple of bags at left luggage and then collected the Royal Worcester from Jenners for Lucille and Desi. With Atticus happily ensconced in his pushchair and me armed with my portable telephone we weaved our way along Princes Street. At the National Gallery we stopped off outside for a ride on a Victorian carousel. Studying it, the painting involved in maintaining it must be considerable. Atticus wanted some lunch so we stopped off at Pizzaland. I felt like a single parent or a Saturday father or just a weekend parent. I looked in to M? (illegible), Virgin and Waterstones before surprising Mother by also looking in to Wilkie's. Yohanan telephoned when we were in the shop and collected us in his car and shortly thereafter we were no sooner Peebles bound. En-route Martha telephoned – 'Would we collect a teapot and cups for Aoidhnait?' The portable phone proved its worth for that alone. It was good fun with us all travelling together and Atticus was really very good. We collected the clock – now chiming away merrily home in The Northlands – so we were really just in and out of Peebles. We stopped off at Lucille and Desi's house at Liberton. Nell's husband and young daughter were there too. I made all the right cooing noises about the house, but crikey £181000. When we move back to Edinburgh God knows what it will be to – certainly it will be a complete change from the Northlands. In the evening the family got together to enjoy a Chinese at Joan's. Atticus and I stayed overnight at Mother's.

22nd December

1971 Oxgangs The standard fayre this morning, papers but no school. Today was the last official day so I guess there'll have been a good few others off too. The big news is that we've got a new telly – yes! That must have been part of Mum and John's mission in to town yesterday. It's good news as our box has been temperamental recently. The bloke arrived to fit it all up for us. Excellent - that's us all sorted for Christmas telly. The other news was that Dad swung by to see us all. It was odd seeing him again. I don't have that father-son relationship with him. His presence is always unsettling and I'm happier when he's not here at Oxgangs. What can I say? It's all pretty sad, but true. After he left I wrote a letter to my pen-pal Peggy Burbank who lives in New York. I'm not quite sure what brought that notion on. In the evening for the first time in a while I had some chips then watched 'Sportsnight with Coleman'. Chelsea beat Spurs 3-2 in the first leg of the League Cup semi-final. Peter Osgood scored the winner.

1972 Oxgangs Brilliant, the last day of work this week at Thomas Graham & Son. I've been doing some thinking. Athletics has become much more important to me during the past month since I left Oxgangs to live at Joan's. Alongside my diary I think I might start keeping a training diary too as I've been going along to Meadowbank Sports Centre regularly over the past four weeks. I'm getting quite serious about it and would like to try to do quite well. So I've taken a small A5 notebook from work and intend to keep a note of all my training alongside my other diary. With it being a Friday and the prospect of Christmas Day next Monday I was quite happy to go in to work today. Although some of the conditions at the office are a bit Dickensian I felt there was a wee bit of the good side of that about too and Roy allowed me to get away quite early just before three o'clock. It was a great feeling walking along Balcarres Street with the long weekend ahead and Christmas at Joan and Darby's. In the evening Paul and I were up at Meadowbank and sneaked in for a game of squash as well as a game of table tennis. It's quite funny as we have to borrow the racquets but the chap on duty gave them to us. Paul stayed overnight so it was back to Porty and a St Andrew's fish 'n chips supper. Heaven.

1973 Portobello Dougie McLean gave me a lift out to Fernieside for the Edinburgh Southern Harriers' Road Relays. Given my dismal distance running ability I'm not sure why but I was given a spot on the Edinburgh Athletic Club Youth B team and I ran okay. We almost pulled off a shock result only losing to the more fancied A team by one second. It may not have made much of a difference but I would have quite fancied running that last leg. Coach Walker gave me a lift back home; I phoned Paul but he had already gone out.

1974 Portobello Bob crashed his mother's car down at North Berwick. It's perhaps unsurprising given the speed he drives at but nevertheless a bit of a shocker. I've made arrangements to meet up with Aileen next Tuesday. *Grand Prix'* was on. I've just heard 'Je t'aime' – it's beautiful.

1975 Portobello I spent the afternoon at Meadowbank sitting talking with people. I watched *Women in Love*. Not much good. No real story.

1976 Portobello I decided to give work (Scottish Council of Social Services) a miss and pottered away with the Triumph Spitfire. I had the open-top down. I took Joan out in it to get the messages. I watched *Grand Prix*.

1977 Portobello I drove my sister Áine and myself out to Livingstone to see Dad. A wet, damp day but I enjoyed passing through the little villages on Edinburgh's back door. Áine was unwell with a pain in her side. Dad was quite impressed with my CV but rightly points out it's light on the qualifications front. Whilst Dad and Bette were out, alongside babysitting Roddy, we put their Christmas decorations up. Back to Oxgangs: I gave Yohanan, Z. and her sister D. a lift to their flat. It's helpful getting £10 from Dad.

1978 Portobello Joan is down with the flu. I picked up some Arcari's ice cream from 99 Portobello High Street. Darby isn't doing anything to help out. I had a couple of drinks at Kilns before going to the nurses' party. I didn't stay long and was in bed by midnight.

1980 Portobello A wild day. A lovely swim down at Portobello Baths except for getting very sore eyes. I loved watching the programme *The Pinch* about the theft of the Stone of Destiny on Christmas Eve 1950 by a group of young Scottish nationalists and the comedic turns as they wended their way northwards taking the Stone across the border back to Scotland. A riveting and charming story and just right for the season of the year.

1981 Portobello It's amazing the difference having a partner at this time of the year makes – the first time since 1978. You're so much busier without even having to try. I saw the birthday girl (Martha) off to work. She was in a cheery mood. I spent an hour at my desk and collected the messages. Margaret Elliot-Ross looked in to see us armed with a bundle of Christmas cards. She was looking well. I managed to buy our Christmas tree in Portobello – the best one in the shop. It's six foot, fairly bushy but cost us a fiver. Gavin Miller asked if I fancied a game of squash. I said no but wondered whether he could give me a lift to take away the last of Martha's stuff from the Gayfield Square flat. In the evening Joan and I enjoyed a documentary on Sean Connery although I would have preferred more interviewing as I found him both interesting and intelligent. I sat up until 1.00 am reading *Bobby Fischer: Profile of a Prodigy* by Frank Brady which I'm enjoying; but still no Martha back from her office party.

1982 Portobello Happy birthday darling girl. Age 24 today. And looking lovelier than ever. It was just a pity you had to go to work. Joan prepared a beautiful tea-table including a home-baked chocolate cake cream sponge all captured for evermore in a photograph or two. I pushed out a good long run in the morning and then spent a happy few hours browsing in the Edinburgh Bookshop at George Street. I bumped into college lecturer John Gilchrist and we had a good blether about South Africa; international athletics coach John Anderson, etc. I managed to buy some Christmas presents including a small carousel for Martha; I hope it doesn't drive her mad. I also bumped into Mrs Swanson and Heather our original neighbours at 6/1 Oxgangs Avenue. It was lovely to speak to them. Gavin qualifies PhD. From Cambridge next month and is off to Zurich. Fantastic. How far he's come. I also met Paul Forbes by accident too. It's a small world. And then Martha at the bus-stop. We had a lovely birthday tea. A very happy evening.

Funny day.
I don't mean I was laughing.
Well I was.
I couldn't go around
With a long face
On your birthday
But. A strange day.
I felt only a very small part
Of today.
Your busy Birth Day.

1983 Powderhall Martha enjoyed her birthday so much she asked me to record it in my journal. When she cheerily got in at 1.30 am from the office party she awoke me and I gave her the moon and stars birthday card I'd made. First thing in the morning I served her a sleepy girl in bed breakfast. Nell popped through to give her a lovely present of a small blue and white Chinese teapot which goes with the colours in the sitting room. Later she surprised her at work with a bouquet of flowers too. And a further surprise as she'd won a bottle of The Famous Grouse whisky in the office party draw. And surprise number three, coming home to a birthday cake with candles; a prawn salad; and fruit cocktail and cream. A day of surprises because Shirley had also called her from Canada at 8.15 am and of course lots of cards and bits 'n bobs from family and friends. All rather lovely and particularly lovely seeing her so very happy and chipper all day. Later in the evening Nell and Richard brought her in a box of chocolates. A 25th birthday to remember although I'd thought it 24 – the number of candles I'd placed on the cake.

1988 Morningside Martha remained very ill all day with this flu virus so we had to cancel the surprise Friday evening dinner party for her. Instead Nell, Richard and Lucille popped round for mincemeat pies and tea. It was actually quite pleasant. At nine o'clock Donald Ross looked round from Craiglea Drive with a bouquet of flowers for her. At lunchtime I met Paul for a bar lunch at The Cockatoo Inn at Millerhill and we then had a few games of snooker. I'm leading 3-2 in our wee series.

1990 Colinton Earlier in the day Mum and I looked in to an antiques fair and then on together to McNaughton's Bookshop for a browse. It's always a little stiff in there. Shortly before nightfall I walked out in the rain to gather in some holly and ivy: Martha has made a lovely decoration for the fire. The season of the year. A pleasant evening out for Martha's birthday. We had some nibbles round at Nell and Richard's along with Desi and Lucille and from Buckstone drove down to Tarvit Street to the New North China Restaurant. Despite having made a booking they had to make up a table to accommodate us. Martha wasn't pleased. However it turned out to be a rather lovely and happy evening.

1993 Colinton *(Martha's Birthday)* Martha got the best possible news for her birthday. The results came through – it's good news. IT'S GREAT NEWS (pregnant). We are so pleased. I spent the day looking after my nieces Caomhog and Lulu; and also Martha's nephews Loki and Timothy (down from Ullapool). A fun adventure day out. We were in Princes Street getting the last of Martha's presents before stopping off at Macdonalds and then on to the Victorian carousel. Good fun. I also took them to the Scottish Gallery of Modern Art. I asked them for their views on the large sculptures outside the gallery - 'A woman with tits.' replied Loki. In the evening we all gathered in the library-dining room for Martha's candle-lit birthday dinner. The boys thought the room was magical. We were joined by Niall Moor; Desi and Lucille; Nell and Richard, alongside Martha's sister.

1994 Colinton It took us the whole morning to get the house and then the *sledge* ready before we headed north for Christmas. I was unable to bring Joan and Aunt Dottle up to house-sit until around lunchtime. The countryside is covered in frost. We met Robbie and Helen at Perthshire; they had been enjoying a lovers' lunch aka the poor man's pleasure. We picked up their Christmas presents. It was like Santa's sledge. The Perth valley was beautiful encased in an incredible white-white frost. At Pitlochry we stopped to feed Atticus and a cup of tea for Martha and thereafter to Drumochter Summit for a pit-stop to enjoy a roll and flask of soup. We turned the car around to enjoy watching the hundreds of deer down from the hill-tops, grazing against a background of snow. It was all the present we could give Martha for her birthday. We arrived at the farm (Wyvis) at five o'clock. Dinner at 7.30 pm. A capon - very nice, with a stuffing of haggis. Later on one of Martha's brothers Peter and partner Aoidhnait joined us for a drink. Some early signs of disharmony I afear, especially on Aoidhnait's side - only 22 and married for less than two years and a little unsatisfied with her lot.

1995 Colinton Despite the snow Mother and John looked in last evening with a wee something for Martha's birthday. They only stayed for an hour but enjoyed dropping by. We made them very welcome. The snows of last night are rapidly disappearing under a steady rain leaving miles of slush; so much so I turned back from my run and did some slow-fasts in the Colinton Dell Railway Tunnel. I quite enjoyed being able to run 'indoors'. The surface is uneven in parts but I wasn't running quickly so in fact it was just right. There was an innate pleasure in keeping dry whilst outside the rain came down persistently - quite miserable out. In the evening we had guests round for Martha's birthday. In company I notice a hint of aggressiveness towards me from her which isn't atypical of our day to day life, giving a slightly distorted view of the world. As ever Nell was lovely. And her new partner M. was sociable too. As usual Lucille and I fell out over something minor. But it's par for the course and later on we were all very relaxed and friendly having a good conversation; when they were leaving I even gave her a light peck on the cheek. Much of the Indian meal was left over probably enough for tomorrow's dinner if I wanted. I feel I'm too bland with my selections but all enhanced by the choices of others which were much hotter and spicier.

1996 Edinburgh/The Northlands I left Mum's and somehow managed to carry eight bags; a chiming old clock (now working); wee Atticus and a pushchair on to the train. A very hard frost throughout the countryside. From the train window I saw two youngsters out in a white field with a model aeroplane. Sheep. Frozen ponds. Cold looking rivers. Frozen fields. Martha met us at Inverness Station. She is 38 today. We had eighteen people round for her birthday. The house could easily accommodate at least three times that for any party. Jan McDonald was over. And then our neighbours Mike and Jan Burns. Robbie; Helen and three kids were round too and stayed over. My father-in-law – Wyvis - thought it expensive to have three separate fires on the go – one in the library; one in the dining room; and one in the sitting room.

23rd December

1971 Oxgangs Paul and I went in to town for much of the day to buy Christmas presents. The town was pretty mobbed but we fair enjoyed ourselves wandering about. We got off the bus at Tollcross and went to Goldbergs before heading down Lothian Road and along Princes Street. We ended up being quite successful and managed to get something for everyone. It was also great being out and about together as we had a good few laughs. It's much better fun shopping in good company; it turns it in to a bit of an adventure. In the evening we all settled back to give the new telly a trial run kicking off with *The Great St Trinian's Train Robbery*. We enjoyed it but you miss Alastair Sim and Joyce Grenfell. Afterwards we watched Brigitte Bardot who was also great.

1972 Portobello Paul and I spent a pretty relaxed day at Joan's. We watched some telly; there was a *Grandstand Special* so we were able to see some of the highlights from the Munich Olympics again including Borzov; Viren; and of course Edinburgh's David Jenkins on the last leg of the 4 x 400 metres relay – brilliant. Mid-afternoon the two of us wandered down to Asda to pick up a wee bit of shopping. It's an amazing store. Tommy Docherty has been poached from the Scotland job to Manchester United and they managed to get a good 1-1 draw with the great Leeds United team. In the evening we sat in by the fire watching *War Wagon* which is a pretty solid Western and then late on a *Parkinson Special* with Bing Crosby. A nice relaxed day to start off the Christmas season.

1973 Portobello I didn't go up to Meadowbank until later today. I did a very good run and in the afternoon did my weights session. I'm giving athletics coach Bill a ring if I don't see him tomorrow. I watched the film *How the West Was Won* – an epic two and a half hours' worth and great stuff – a history lesson really.

1975 Portobello Today was a very lazy sort of a morning; still I am on holiday. Davie Reid phoned me and I went up to Meadowbank. We sat around for an hour listening to the 'Pros' and the bookies arguing about the professional athletics and the upcoming New Year Sprint. They were all pretty animated; it was fun and interesting being a fly on the wall. I thereafter did an average sort of a session. I'm feeling a bit of a cold coming on which is a bugger given I've got this big race at Cosford. In the evening I relaxed at home enjoying watching the enigmatic *Lawrence of Arabia*, what a man; what a life; what a film. Magnificent stuff. He's Grandma Joan's hero and she's suggested I *read The Seven Pillars of Wisdom* from her library.

1977 Portobello I managed to work away on Accounts and enjoyed the satisfaction of working through a financial position. After lunch, a wee tootle up to Safeways for a few messages including seasonal bottles for Joan and then up to Meadowbank. There was no rush today: Dennis Davidson had dropped by the house this morning to say no rub tonight. I did a circuit and then for fun did some weights. I lifted about 140 lbs above my head. I was quite surprised and pleased with that. Afterwards I did a hill session up on Arthurs Seat before running round it. I got caught in a downpour of rain. Before my shower I bench-pressed 130 lbs. An evening in. I've a sore throat so took some penicillin. With the Commonwealth Trials only six months away I'm keen to have less time off as I seem to lose months every year because of all the infections I'm always picking up. I sat up late in front of a warm coal fire watching television with Perry Como's *An Olde Englishe Christmas* getting me in the mood for the best time of the year.

1978 Portobello I looked into Oxgangs before going to watch *Superman*. The story was very poor.

1981 Portobello A few hill runs on School Brae and a mad-cap dash to Safeways before going out to Oxgangs to join Mum for a visit to Dr Motley's for coffee and a mince pie. I was in town to pick up some last minute presents for people – just something small for everyone including diaries. The snow was tumbling down. I successfully got Martha's main present – a smart Donkey jacket at George IV Bridge; it may be too small but will be a snug fit. Whilst there I bumped into the eccentric Mr (Paul) Forbes. Joan made a lovely job of Martha's birthday tea - some lovely fish and vegetables – a chocolate birthday cake and a fresh cream gateaux before we went out for Martha's birthday treat, 'Jack and the Beanstalk' at the Kings Theatre. It had its moments. And we enjoyed ourselves. We arrived home – eventually – but only after trudging through the snow from Duddingston Golf Course into the face of a biting wind. Once home, Martha began her packing for The Northlands whilst I wrapped up several presents. Late late to bed.

1982 Portobello Martha and I went up to town – her to work, me to pick up a sledge as a Christmas present for my nephews Kirk and Kent. Once back home Yohanan (brother) and the boys arrived. It was like the madhouse. Feeding them. Exchanging presents. Letting Yohanan have a whirlwind tour of my records. It was a shame he had to leave at 1.00 pm as it would have been nice to have them here all afternoon. I tested out my fitness with a 2.5 mile time-trial. Considering I did it in my tracksuit I thought it fair. In the evening I sat contentedly in my room with a sherry and the lights off with just the warm orange glow of the fire. Martha is through in the sitting room.

1983 Powderhall The slight cold I've had for the past month is now full blown: a bugger as I've been looking forward to four days of freedom from the Scottish Episcopal Church. I awoke feeling listless with aches, pains and a sore throat. It was a wet morning and I picked up my first puncture cycling to work at Hamilton Place Stockbridge. It was a slightly awkward spot to wheel the bike along the Water of Leith and up to the Grosvenor Crescent office. There was no work as the computer folk had all the ledgers so I sat and read 'The Scotsman'. In the late Friday afternoon I saw Martha and Nell onto the train off to the Highlands for the Christmas celebrations. I'd prepared some snacks for them. I spent an hour hoovering and tidying the flat then repaired my puncture before heading down to Joan's. I spoke to old Frank: he said the people upstairs look in to see him with presents on Christmas Day – good to hear that someone's thinking of him. At Porty I just missed my cousin David Ross handing in the cards. There's a nice coal fire going. I sat in bed reading. The dog was glad of my company. Unfortunately Joan is going down with a bad cold. She's had a terrible run of bad luck this winter.

1984 Powderhall It was just as well I didn't join the Sunday training group at Gullane as I was just too darn busy. Both Martha and I were getting our bags ready. At lunchtime I saw her on to her bus at St Andrew's Square, Highland-bound. Back at the flat, for no accountable reason other than I'm a worrier I felt uneasy hoping nothing would happen to the bus, etc. I staggered down to Porty with all my bags. Áine; Spieler; Yohanan and his boys Kirk and Kent swung round to pick me up. We took a detour via Stobsmills House Gorebridge. Margaret and the household were all busy except Robert Spinrad. Frances was making sweets; Eloise was polishing the table; whilst Margaret was decking the hall with greenery; and David was writing out Christmas cards. A lovely festive household straight out of Dickens. At Oxgangs it was great fun putting the boys to bed with much hysterical laughter between them, their dad Yohanan and me. After our meal and TV, Áine and I had a good going discussion with me arguing that Jimmy Boyle's troubles were partly the result of his environment and socialisation process; whereas Áine was saying it was genetic – then not – then not really knowing. It generated much heat.

1986 Powderhall Welcome to the new style diary. Although it won't actually be a diary, but something more than that. I don't quite know what it might yet evolve into – perhaps more of an everyday or commonplace book. We'll see how it progresses. But whilst I intend to fill it with the usual diary notes but on top of that I intend to paste in small articles which I like – fashion, sport, etc – anything or anyone who inspires me. Today was crisp and bright and frosty. I ran in the morning and shopped in the afternoon. Yesterday was Martha's 28th birthday and a happy one. She was working whilst I was on holiday. I met her in the evening. We enjoyed a pleasant salad at The Filmhouse then spur of the moment watched *Jagged Edge* which was quite brilliant. Mum sometimes judges films by how quickly the time goes by. Well, time flew. We both enjoyed it. For her birthday and Christmas I've bought her some Art Nouveau jewellery – matching earrings and a brooch. She likes them which makes me feel good. Nell gave her a bright scarf/shawl which she hasn't had off her back all day and other small items too.

1988 Morningside A windy evening out the flat bay window. It's been raw and wet all day. I took Mum and John down to Safeways at Morningside to do the Christmas shopping: it was so busy we even had to queue to get into the car park and that at 8.30 am! Whilst inside the shop we saw Nettie who talked to Mum. She looks wonderful for 70. The poor woman was in tears remembering her darling only daughter Pam who died quite young in her teens from cancer leaving Nettie and her husband bereft. Such a terrible thing and of course Pam was an only child too. I delivered some presents to (half-brother) Roddy and Bette and have invited him through for a game of snooker during the holidays. Late afternoon I had a rub at Denis's and a bowl of soup at Joan's. Margaret Elliot-Ross looked in – handy for me to pass on my Christmas cards and a copy of Patrick Leigh-Fermor. These past few evenings I've enjoyed reading Washington Irvine's *Old Christmas* getting me in the mood for the season of the year.

1989 Ullapool I couldn't suffer Martha's sister's rudeness and insults any longer so walked out. She'd made me very unwelcome in the house so I just upped and left. I could have chosen a better time than a Friday evening as I was effectively stranded in the village 40 miles from civilisation with only mountains rivers and lochs in-between, having to sleep out rough before getting some chocolate for breakfast and the first bus out, getting off at Smith's Garage at Contin Village. I managed to thumb a lift to The Northlands where I had coffee and a snack at Deas Café and read the Saturday morning newspapers before walking the uphill three miles to the farm. It was sunny and the views down on to the Cromarty Firth were wonderful. I was within 100 yards of Wyvis when Martha arrived from Ullapool in the car; she was glad to see me and gave me a lift the remaining way. My legs were sore, as was my shoulder from my heavy bag. An adventure. In the evening young Gavin and I peeled the chestnuts for the stuffing.

1990 Morningside I've just waved Martha off to Perth; The Northlands and Ullapool. She's loaded down - a Santa Claus on wheels, with presents galore. I'm reading Jean Gategbo's *Fragments of Alice through the Looking Glass*. It's a book I bought years ago in Canada at the 1978 Commonwealth Games in Edmonton. I'm enjoying it greatly, especially so following on from watching Denis Potter's play 'How He Got To Wonderland' which was on television earlier in the week, all about Martha and the Reverend Charles Dodgson. My sister Áine and husband Spieler are now not coming for Christmas dinner after all. I think the rest of the family are a bit brassed off about that. However. In the morning I enjoyed a long run with the usual Sunday group along the Water of Leith. I spent the afternoon tidying up the house in preparation for Mum, John and Yohanan arriving tomorrow for our *Country Christmas*. The afternoon was stormy with a high wind. It was delightful watching the cats especially Biff chasing after a dozen leaves a-blowing in different directions. In their first year they're so full of life. Above the wood on the opposite bank of the Water of Leith lots of birds were circling in the sky.

1993 Colinton The snow came this afternoon. Unbelievably, Martha; her sister; and the boys Loki and Thor set out at 7.00 pm for Perthshire with the turkey and Christmas presents. They got back to West Mill at midnight. I was unamused.

1994 Inverness I spent the late morning-early afternoon in Leakey's second-hand bookshop. He's now moved into an impressive former church building making for a very large shop indeed. After looking at Bert Barrett's Edinburgh West Port Bookshop earlier I've made up my mind to one day open such a shop of my own.

1995 Colinton Yohanan and Sinéadte dropped by with a birthday present for Martha and a Dennis the Menace jumper for Atticus. As Martha says they're very generous. I spoke to Martha about the disappointing way she'd behaved toward me last evening so of course we've fallen out. I went off to paint the back bedroom with a 1½ inch brush - very therapeutic! In the background I had the excellent 'James Taylor Live' album playing. Atticus (aged 19 months) jumped into Bonnyrigg Pool on his own - a rather lovely surprise - week by week he's coming on. Last evening Nell and M. were impressed by his vocabulary. We drove down to Áine's with £30 for the kids but they were out. Atticus and I dropped by Joan's.

Mother was there too. Áine looked a bit despondent sitting in the far corner but brightened up when she saw Atticus. Joan was working on a Christmas card for Atticus; it has a snowman on it. It was lovely sharing this early eve of Christmas yet to come with the four generations together: I savoured the moment. Back at West Mill we relaxed in sitting up late with the newspapers and television cosy in the warmth of our lovely cottage with the festive holiday season all in front of us.

Christmas Eve

1971 Oxgangs A fun and very different Christmas Eve. I got the bus down to Baird's Newsagent's Morningside early on with the Blades girls to do my papers. It was a breeze doing my paper-run this morning. I sensed anyone I came across was enjoying this special time of the year. Back home 6/2 feels alive with a good atmosphere; everyone is in a good mood, excited and enjoying the season of goodwill. We tidied the house up a wee bit with 'White Christmas' and Bing Crosby on in the background. Thereafter we chilled out for a wee while. Oxgangs and home feels good; it's great being part of a family. In the late afternoon we all took the 16 bus in to Princes Street then got the number 24 bus to Stockbridge to 14 Dean Park Street and Nana Pepys's. I think that's the first time I've mentioned Nana in this year's diary and also the first time I've seen her this year: it's a complete contrast to seeing Nana and Darby every week. It all came about through Dad looking in to see us on Wednesday. It was nice to see her and she was glad to see us all; it probably cheered her up no end to have a full house on Christmas Eve. We all got ready for the Christmas Eve party and just walked through Stockbridge and along to Henderson Row to Pat and Ronnie Browne's for the party. We had a great time there; as well as the Browne's, all the Ross's were there too. Their New Town house is fantastic; similar to Andy and Margaret's next door - it's just a wee bit different from Oxgangs. It's great being part of the extended family. I like all the Ross's and Brown's. After midnight and in to Christmas Day Ronnie Browne gave us all a lift home to Oxgangs in his big Jaguar. We all managed to squeeze in; it was very good of him but he wouldn't hear of us going for a late night bus or taking an expensive taxi. Happy Christmas everyone. That's me written my diary; apart from Simon the cat, I'm the last man standing: I'm off to bed now.

1972 Portobello After a delicious breakfast from Joan of bacon, eggs and mushrooms, Paul and I went up to train at Meadowbank. We trained in the morning with Mr Walker's group. When they all left we had a plate of chips and then spent the afternoon talking with John Anderson and his group of international athletes. We're a bit cheeky asking to join in but Mr Anderson's pretty good about it. We enjoyed ourselves. In the morning we ran 4 x 600 metres with a 4 minute interval in 107; 102; 96; and 108 seconds. In the afternoon I did some weight training with Dick Williamson then 4 x 4 x 60 metres back to back with 2 minutes recovery in between the sets. I then did 40 sit-ups. Later on I saw Dad and then watched the telly including a scary *A Ghost Story for Christmas* by M.R. James called 'A Warning for the Curious'. Oh, I've just seen my Christmas stocking from Mum which she must have passed on to Joan and Darby when I was at Meadowbank today.

1973 Portobello It didn't seem to be so bad a Monday morning at work as it was Christmas Eve. And because it was the office Christmas lunch (which I couldn't afford to attend) because of the two hour break I managed to travel home with Darby from Waugh & Son Butchers at Morningside to Portobello for our lunch together. They let us away early at four o'clock. In the evening I'd missed everyone at Meadowbank but Stuart Gillies and his wife gave Paul and me a lift to the Edinburgh Athletic Club dance at Musselburgh. Mark, Paul and I got stoned. I got off with Petrina. I also necked. Dougie gave me a lift home from Mountcastle.

1974 Portobello I arrived at the Post Office at nine o'clock (student holiday job) to collect a pretty heavy bag of Christmas post. I managed to drop one of my bundles in the mud and rain – stupid beggar. I managed to do some training but was struggling somewhat, followed by a shower and visit to the physio asking him to focus on my tight shoulder from working as a postman. Mum and Áine were down giving Joan a hand with the Christmas preparations before we gave them a lift home to Oxgangs. I met Aileen Gordon at the top of the road and Darby gave us and Paul a lift down to Musselburgh for the annual Edinburgh Athletic Club Christmas Dance. However, after a threat that the police were going to raid the premises we left at a quarter to ten taking a taxi out to Bob's at Bangholm Terrace along with a couple of Trinity Academy girls including Ann Clarkson, Aileen and myself. We all went along to the Christmas Carol Service which I enjoyed. Bob kindly gave each of us a lift home. Oh Mike Farrell says there isn't too good a field for the 400 metres at RAF Cosford.

1975 Portobello Mr C. (Campbell) gave me a rub first thing – he's a great lad. I picked up a few Christmas messages then lay about watching *Star Trek* – a damn good programme. I was in at Dr Motley's then gave my sister Áine a lift down to Henderson Row to Margaret Ross's. I picked my brother Yohanan up and we looked in to see Nana Pepys at Dean Park Street; she was very glad to see the two of us drop by. And from there to visit Dad – he was steamboats – but so? When dropping Yohanan off at Oxgangs, Gail Blades stopped to speak – we've agreed to meet up for a drink sometime.

I Started Early-Took My Dog

I started Early-Took my Dog-

And visited the Sea-

The Mermaids in the Basement

Came out to look at me-

And Frigates-in the Upper Floor

Extended Hempen Hands-

Presuming Me to be a Mouse-

Aground-upon the Sands

Emily Dickinson

1976 Portobello A Christmas Eve to remember. The weather was remarkably fine, bright and mild. I drove the Triumph Spitfire down the East Lothian coastline to Gullane. I ran a good session on the sands, with the dog skipping along beside me. On Christmas Eve it felt magical to once again be by the sea. On such a special day it felt good to be alive and healthy and outside in the fresh air and to be out running. I wanted to affix the moment in my mind's-eye. After the session it was with a dreamy sense of an inner glow and satisfaction that I walked back along the sands to the car, parked high on the cliff. On the way I glimpsed a couple of boats gliding along the Forth upon a calm sea; and although the weather was far finer and kinder I thought of (Robert Louis) Stevenson's poem Christmas at Sea:

Christmas at Sea

'...The bells upon the church were rung with a mighty jovial cheer;
For it's just that I should tell you how (of all the days in the year)
This day of our adversity was blessed Christmas morn And the house above the coastguard's was the house where I was born...'

I visited old John Macpherson before going on to a Watchnight service at Davidsons Mains.

1977 Portobello On a less happy note I awoke with a ghastly sore throat and a burning session in my chest. It's a bugger with the AAA Indoor Championships next month and my debut over 800 metres. I seem to collect so many colds and viruses but more worrying still is my inability to throw them off. It's my biggest flaw and my greatest weakness. The doctor was closed for the holiday but I managed to get some Ampicillin from Dr Hislop. I took it very easy just sitting in reading David Niven's *The Moon's A Balloon*. After tea we played bagatelle before taking Christmas cards and some Harvey's Bristol Cream to the Ross's at 6 Henderson Row and then the same to the Walker family at 54 Claremont Crescent. Coach Walker's wife Kay served us up some red wine and mincemeat pies; we sat around chatting with the kids until eleven o'clock before we left to go to the midnight service; once again it was packed out and was so busy we had to sit opposite each other on aisle pews. I didn't get home until one o'clock in the morning. A Happy Christmas to one and all.

1978 Portobello Well here we are once again - Christmas Eve - my favourite time of the year, with it all to come. At lunchtime, in pretty awful conditions I ran a pleasingly good, solitary track session at Meadowbank. John and Áine were down for the afternoon. Thereafter Darby and I ran them across to Henderson Row to Maggie's and then onward to Oxgangs. I ended up running the seven miles home down to Portobello. Running through Arthurs Seat on almost the darkest evening of the year was quite miserable - the wind was howling with a steady rain but after a warm bath I sat in front of a lovely coal fire soaking up the heat *watching El Cid* and feeling quite content and happy - pure luxury after being out in such wild weather and feeling I'd done something quite positive.

To truly enjoy being indoors you really do need to have experienced the raw outdoors. On our way to the church service we spotted Gavin Miller sitting alone in the Roxburgh Hotel glancing out contemplatively upon Charlotte Square whilst drinking coffee and sitting reading the Sunday Telegraph. There was only one other old man sitting reading too – straight out of Dickens or perhaps a William Trevor short story – the lonely and sometimes sad lives of the late middle aged bachelor. In the season of the year when you feel being on your own most of all. We were actually too late arriving at the church doors – not a seat rather than a bed to be found at the inn. Bed at 1.00 am. Bon soir.

1979 Portobello This morning I had a flaming argument with Joan which upset me for the rest of the day. After lunch I spent much of the morning by the fire enjoying Orson Welles in *Treasure Island* before wandering wistfully around the town. I haven't felt like buying Christmas presents for anyone. I thought Gavin Miller might phone, but no: I wonder what he's doing, poor soul. I'm going to read a Graham Greene novel but may have a quick look at a text-book first. Later I'm looking forward to watching *Alan Price in Concert*. There was a letter in the post from Sally written in the early hours of

Christmas Eve:

1.00 a.m. 24th December (1979)
The North West Coast

Samuel, my love,

I am lying in bed and have been thinking about you for at least two hours. I am feeling communicative, mainly because I have been drunk rather a lot which weakens my inhibitions and also because Maurice took me out for a meal tonight and I am feeling guilty because you did not know. I dislike dishonesty, not that I knew when I was talking to you, but none the less, it is unfair. I miss you a lot, not all the time but at periods when we would normally talk to one another about one another, especially at this time of the night. Our telephone conversation was an anti-climax for me because I wanted you to say you missed me, or the like, but as usual, I was not prepared to give the same commitment. After putting the phone down I felt a bit lost and confused. What did you feel? In the morning it will be Xmas Eve and the final preparations will be made. I have not sent you a present because I don't know what I would like to give you so, I shall resolve the problem anon, somehow, I have one idea, we shall see how acceptable it is when I see you.

I want to come down to Edinburgh on the 31st, so I shall see you then. I am not sure what time my train arrives but it is not that necessary à ce moment! I am getting tired and my concentration is failing so I shall love you and have you until such time as I see you. The night is dark and deep and I can feel you in my mind.

Long may this continue, my love, and thank you for your card.

All love

Sally

X Whee Wheeeeeeeeee!

1980 Portobello

Joan and I took a bus along to Safeways to get in some last minute Christmas groceries. Despite being up at Princes Street for some hours I did nothing constructive towards buying Christmas presents other than buying Yohanan a pipe and young Roddy (age 7) a copy of *Stevenson's A Child's Garden of Verse*. Dad and Bett's extended family picked me up and I spent a few hours with them out at Livingstone. Dad dropped me off at the West End although we sat in the car talking for a few hours. He's very supportive of me and my current unhappiness. I dashed into the House of Fraser at 5.55 pm emerging minutes later with Christmas plates for my sister Áine and Margaret Elliot-Ross. Joan has been busy all day and is still through in the kitchen (9.00 pm). I've retired to bed reading Charles Dickens' *'A Christmas Carol'* before drifting off to sleep.

1981 Portobello/The Northlands

A very busy morning after seeing a laden Martha off to work. I spent the morning wrapping presents and then filling up her stocking; preparing food for the train; a quick bath; dropping a box off at her flat, before staggering up to Waverley Station to join a very long queue for train tickets. When Martha arrived she was like a drowned rat from the sleety-snow falling outside in Princes Street. She was obviously a bit tired and slightly grumpy but her smile broke through. The train was full and the guard jammed us in like sardines so we appreciated our good fortune in finding a seat together to Perth. However when we changed to join the Inverness bound train we had to sit apart – but at least got a seat each, all down to Martha running to catch the train; t'others from Edinburgh ended up standing for the whole way. The train chuntered through some bonnie Highland landscape with everything painted white. Towards and through Drumochter Summit we looked out at the deer down from the high summits to graze on the lower slopes – there must have been a few hundred thousand pounds worth over a ten mile stretch! The train was more or less on time. Martha's brother Robbie was very good coming in to collect us at Inverness Station. We laughed all the way to Northlands for an amazingly warm welcome with a roaring coal fire and dozens of presents around the family Christmas tree. I was quite excited about playing Santa Claus to my pal.

1982 Portobello I spent the morning writing Christmas cards and wrapping presents. For once Aunt Dottle was doing some real work about the place. Around 1.30 pm Martha arrived home to get packed. She was a bit out of sorts and then told ME that I was sulking! We struggled up Durham Road with her bags and parcels as well as a box of chocolates for Jimmy Brash fortunately bumping into Mrs B en-route. We arrived early at the bus station but as they were putting on three buses - two extra coaches - which meant Martha got away sharply. It felt strange once she'd left and the coach pulled out of St Andrew's Square. I didn't bother going down to Henderson Row to deliver cards to the Ross's and instead just came home. Despite all the goodies – chocolate cake, etc. I just had a small wholesome tea. In my snug bedroom I sketched out a small poem for Martha.

Christmas Away

I've got your card.

It's a little part.

Of you.

Here with me.

This Christmas Eve.

It's comfortable.

The fire glowing orange.

Dim, lamp-lit.

Television burning. Papers and magazines.
And books by my side.
Wish it were you.
Slumped here
In my big old armchair.
In the seclusion
Of our little room
Thinking. Thoughts of you.
You. And wheels
Flying through the night
Like Father Christmas
Carrying
The most important package in all the world.
The chimes of the clock
Stretching out the miles between us.
Strange though. I feel closer to you than ever
My darling, darling girl. Merry Christmas

Come 7.30 pm I went out and ran six or seven miles. It was quite fun on this very special evening in the calendar year running through the streets taking in the magic of Christmas Eve Edinburgh street life – lots of taxis were going up and down – families travelling together in cars, out and about delivering gifts to friends, families and loved ones – there was a crowd of teenagers in party spirits emerging from The Sheep's Heid Inn in Duddingston Village and about to hit the town but no sign amongst them of my early morning running partner Steven – I hope he's out enjoying himself and not in with just his mum. The Esso petrol station forecourt was very busy with drivers filling up their tanks – a small kiddie was out running to the chip shop for the family's tea – a middle-aged couple stood with cases awaiting a taxi – a group of office workers were coming away from an office meal and drinks night out – a couple of teenage girls in jeans and jackets were off to meet pals – a myriad of kitchen windows were lit up with women busily working away –

I got a friendly wave from Stuart Gray (from Oxgangs) who was driving a Corporation bus – a couple of elderly women at the foot of Durham Road emerged from a Mini car and were carrying presents whilst being greeted at the garden gate by a middle-aged man. And then it was back home for a bath and changed and a relaxing Harvey's Bristol Cream sherry and some TV. Martha phoned at 9.45 pm. She'd arrived safely. Tucked up in bed I listened in to the radio and an Edinburgh church service.

1983 Portobello I made the fire for Joan – now that she's 75 it's something which I feel Aunt Dottle should be doing for her these days. And after porridge some housework – hoovering, etc. Nothing much more needs to be done in terms of food preparation for the big day but I picked up a few messages from Benson's at the top of the road and also walked the dog. In the afternoon, despite it being wet and miserable, I took a contemplative stroll down to Portobello. I picked up a Bertrand Russell book. I enjoyed looking in the lit up shop windows with people milling around rushing about to buy last minute Christmas presents. A quiet evening in, but pleasant to look out the front room bay window at carol singers in Durham Road, although they didn't stop by our door. The TV was poor other than *Cider with Rosie*. Martha called later in the evening from the Highlands – soft-voiced and genuinely missing me. I miss her. I sat up in bed reading Graham Swift's *Waterland* – I'm persevering with it but no thumbs up from me – at least yet.

1984 Portobello An unaccustomed sharpness in the air today made worse by a snell wind. We all breakfasted together and then I took off on my seasonal travels bumping into Mrs Brash. She was telling me her son and family have returned from South Africa. He's basically got around six weeks to try to find a new job back here in Edinburgh. At eleven o'clock I did a wee session at Meadowbank with Ewan McAslan. I enjoyed chatting with him. Afterwards Bill Walker gave me a lift home. A spot of lunch and then out to Oxgangs followed by a half hour jog. It was the last episode of *The Box of Delights* which has been wonderful with all the right ingredients for Christmas – there's a deep mysteriousness to the book. I'd handed in some golf balls to Lee: the silly bugger had put his hand through the glass pane in the kitchen door the previous evening in a fit of temper. He'd been drinking and popping pills then to add to his misery had phoned the love of his life, Doreen, who's upped sticks to make a new life for herself in Canada. His mother Julie was unamused. It ended up with him getting stitches at the hospital at 3.00 a.m. On the way home I stopped off at the Playhouse to buy some Meatloaf tickets for Martha's brother Tief. A relaxed evening in. My sister Áine's done a right job of the vegetables. And husband Spieler was here until 8.00 pm. Joan, Aunt Dottle and I sat watching a documentary on Placido Domingo. I was surprised to discover that he's not particularly temperamental at all. I telephoned Martha. Good news – she managed to retrieve her lost bag but it all seems very suspicious – other people's clothes in there too.

1985 Powderhall

Darby

Darby,
I hardly give you a thought now.
It's difficult to believe
How easily I've let you slip out of my life.
It's six years back, come New Year's Day
And
I hardly give you a thought

I just drift along
Consuming. Life.
Books. And friendship. And food.
And all. And all.
And
I hardly give you a thought.

How do I forget?
Pocket monies each and every day of the week.
And that Rangers strip on my birthday.

Yon tracksuit that Christmas.
And running spikes come summer
And a giant egg each and every Easter.
Yet Darby
I hardly give you a thought

Only now and then when I flick through an old diary
Or visit Joan
Or Like today, when passing these rare and becoming rarer
Butcher shops, loaded with Christmas turkeys
That I ever seem to give you a thought

All my days you were a constant
A constant friend And grandfather. And
A grand storyteller.
A constant source of warmth. And optimism - Maybe the coupon'll be up this week!
And yet. I hardly give you a thought

But Darby
Maybe that's just because
I miss you
So very much.

1986 Oxgangs It's 10.30 pm but feels much earlier. I'm sitting in my old Oxgangs bedroom that was mine between 1958 and 1972. Outside I can hear the wind gusting. It's been gradually building up force all day. I'm an hour back from playing snooker with Lee. Quite enjoyable – he's on his merry way in both senses. Martha left for The Northlands at lunchtime. Last evening I stayed with her at her flat. We swapped stockings and sat by the tree opening them. Her's to me very practical. Mine to her, impractical. She laughed at the 'Spitting Image' plastic puppet of David Owen with David Steel in his top pocket. I received some delightful presents from her – a very classy Crabtree & Evelyn shaving set complete with fine brush razor soap and moustache comb, no less. Also the new pen that I'm writing this journal entry with and an Elmore Leonard novel as well as a copy of Peter Akroyd's *Hawksmoor*. Also some chocolates; a telephone message pad; diaries; a hand-warmer for my golf outings; a mug, etc. Everything a winner. John has fitted the cassette-player in my car. In return I've bought him a Marks and Spencer jersey. Earlier I'd looked into Joan's for a bowl of soup. Aunt Dottle was there too. Joan has painted a wonderful Christmas card for my niece Caomhog. I left a card for her with £20 enclosed. I also bought a baby (pram) suit which is quite exquisite.

1988 Morningside As is often the way the Christmas Eve preparations were good fun. Mother and John were down at my flat all day which was nice and I enjoyed their company and I guess just being able to share in my good fortune of owning such a lovely old Morningside flat with its large bay-windowed sitting room and the views out across the city and to Arthurs Seat and the Braid Hills. After helping out all morning they were able to relax for the rest of the day all settled in by the newly installed Victorian fireplace with gas fire, enjoying eating and drinking. Martha was out; then in; then off to The Northlands, despite still being ill with this ongoing cold-flu virus.

1989 Home Comfort Farm The Northlands (12.30 pm) Martha; father-in-law Wyvis and wife; and Martha's youngest brother are all down in The Northlands at the Sunday church service. Martha's brother Douglas is in bed. I'm sitting by a glowing fire in the farmhouse sitting room watching Bob Hope and Bing Crosby in *Road to Utopia*. Outside the window the weather is damp with a slight drizzle but it remains mild for the season of the year. Earlier this morning the wind was gusting and with Wyvis sitting so high up on the hill it's particularly noticeable. I've got a slight cold but managed a half hour jog this morning. A clean shave – it's amazing the difference a fresh new blade does for a few days' growth, leaving you feeling like a new man. Sitting here on my own I feel wonderfully relaxed and at one with the world – in a semi-meditative state of mind. Having only had an hour's sleep in Ullapool the evening before I slept like a log – the best sleep of 1989. I fell asleep as soon as my head hit the pillow. When I got up for a pee I'd thought it was the early hours of the morning only to find it was eight o'clock. The night had passed just like that. Last evening I telephoned Joan and Aunt Dottle both of whom were chirpy but Joan's down with an infection. They had received the gift of a turkey from Martha's brother Robbie - actually a present from Wyvis, home-reared here on the farm. Áine had taken delivery from Helen of the PMR. Helen had thought Áine quite posh - it must have been the big black Rover car rather than her Oxgangs accent! I also phoned Oxgangs - Mum was in the shower so I spoke to John.

Later (9.00 pm) Martha and I have spent the last half hour reading aloud the Christmas Eve part of Susan Hill's *'Lanterns across the Snow'* which I bought two years ago but had never got around to reading. I'd also given my sister Áine a copy too. I notice we're past the midnight hour. Christmas no longer excites me quite the way it once did. As a child it was always the very best day of the year and greatly anticipated - that indescribable feeling of finding your Christmas stocking at the foot of your bed and reaching out feeling the misshapen presents contained inside. Often over the years I've heard Mum say you don't feel the same way about Christmas when you get older - to a certain extent she's right, but straight out of Dickens Joan's always been very good at keeping the season of the year. Earlier in the evening we enjoyed a lovely special Christmas Eve meal through in the conservatory. It's the first such occasion it's been used for this purpose. Wyvis's wife served up a salmon caught from their stretch of the Cromarty Firth earlier in the season in July, followed by a Christmas chocolate log which Martha had made earlier in the day - it almost snookered me. Gavin is away to bed early but is too excited - yet - to get to sleep. Douglas is away to The Northlands for a night out. The four of us - Wyvis and wife; Martha and I are about to settle down to watch an adaptation of Susan Hill's *The Woman in Black*.

1990 Morningside (8.00 am) Martha arrived in the Highlands okay. I telephoned last evening but she was out at a carol service.

Later I collected Mum from her work at Morningside at 4.30 pm buying in some last minute almonds from the local Morningside health shop - the poor shop assistant who served me looked anything but healthy. Yohanan arrived at lunchtime; earlier in the morning the two of us had visited the twins, Lee and Ricky and

Ricky's two excited kids – we gave them a small present each. In the afternoon Yohanan was outside happily washing my car whilst I continued being a commis-chef making preparations for Christmas Day. Mum and John stayed in the master bedroom with its en-suite facilities. Mother liked the little touches – the flowers, the bedside-reading, etc. comparing it to the Queen at Christmas. Yohanan occupied the spare single room upstairs much to his great delight whilst I had 'Janey's Room' which is bright and spacious with its two opposite Velux windows facing to the north and to the south. We had a simple Christmas Eve meal of pizza; baked potato; salad, etc. Later on Yohanan was out with the 'J. machine' (girlfriend) arriving back fu' shortly before the midnight bells rang out.

1991 Colinton (6.45 am) I didn't get much sleep last evening as I was preparing Christmas stockings for Yohanan; John; Mum; Joan and Aunt Dottle who are all coming to stay over to share in my country Christmas in the city here at West Mill. I'd also put in a good shift cleaning and tidying the house but fitted in *Broadway Danny Rose* which I enjoyed. I had no joy buying a turkey at Marks and Spencer so the pressure is on – part of the reason for me getting up so early – or should I say they were sold out of the large ones yesterday so I'm off to town now. Martha is safely ensconced at Home Comfort Farm.

1992 Colinton Martha is safely ensconced in the bosom of the family home at Wyvis, The Northlands. Yesterday the usual crowd – Nell and Richard; Lucille and Desi; and Martha and I went out to Mackenzie's Restaurant, Colinton to celebrate her birthday – a lovely evening amongst long-standing good friends.

1993 Colinton Like many generations before us the boys (Martha's nephews Loki and Timothy down from Ullapool) and I had a wonderful time sledging down the 9th hole at the Merchants Golf Course. With the steepness of the hill it's real daredevil stuff. The lads have plenty of chutzpah and get up and go. Martha and her sister spent all day on the preparations for our Christmas Eve special meal but also with a view towards Christmas Day too. Yohanan dropped by for a coffee, as did Mum and John during the afternoon. Martha and I are probably going to go along to the Watchtower Service at St Mary's Cathedral. I don't think I've ever seen so many presents under a Christmas tree. Bloody ridiculous.

Later We went to the service at St Mary's but found it overly long. The communion dragged. I had one of my occasional energy bursts making me very restless. As a boy I couldn't stand still hopping from foot to foot. It's no wonder I got into bother as a youngster. Bed not long after we returned home to West Mill, in the very early hours of Christmas morning.

1994 Home Comfort Farm The Northlands Good news, the antibiotics are starting to kick in.

1995 Colinton I sat up until 3.00 am into Christmas morn reading rattling off *A Judge's Diary* by Gordon Stott. In the late 1960s and early 1970s I sometimes delivered newspapers from Baird's Newsagent's Morningside Drive to his large home at Midmar Gardens with its enchanting garden pond with the large goldfish that Fiona Blades and I used to sneak round to look at on early sun-kissed summer mornings. I've thoroughly enjoyed his memories – an intelligent, courteous and despite his brilliance, a modest man too. In some respects he reminds me of our director Bob Maslin – a man immediately able to recognise both the principle and the point of any issue or argument. I particularly enjoyed the early pieces in the book when he was still the Lord Advocate but I was less keen when he returned to being a judge again where I was occasionally bored with some of the innumerable divorce proceedings. But there was much that I could identify with and I greatly enjoyed his commentaries on Edinburgh, much of it still of course very recognisable – her citizens; his love of literature and reading and the little crits as well as descriptions of some earlier television programmes, but mostly I guess I just enjoyed soaking up the experience of a shared older Edinburgh that passed me by, but one of which I was an integral part of too, but as a young boy and then as a lad finding my way in the capital. Atypically my sister Áine said she would look by but never did. Not that I was either up nor down about that but in some respects we'd stayed in for her. Any more fluttering's of snow and we could have a white Christmas – there's a cloudless sky and it's cold. So much so I just decided to do a running session in the Colinton Dell former railway tunnel. A sheltered, enjoyable experience once again but at this time of the day there were one or two walkers out as well as a couple of dogs. Tristan looked by just as Atticus was going off to his bed – he was delivering a wee present from his family. It was good to see him so happy and in such good form – I think he was unaware that my boss is leaving Midlothian Council - that would have made him even cheerier as he's been a thorn in the contractor's flesh and I've had to try to steer a middle and conciliatory road bridging the gap between them. This evening we sat down to a lovely Christmas Eve meal. Martha said that in some ways she missed being with her family tonight but in other respects was glad to be out of it too, to enjoy a slightly quieter time here at West Mill.

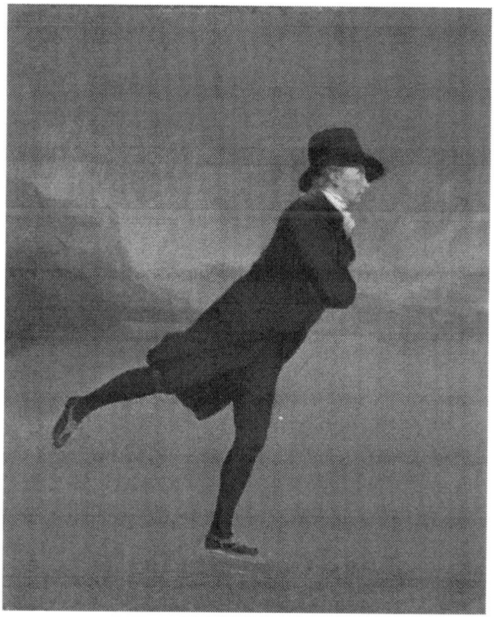

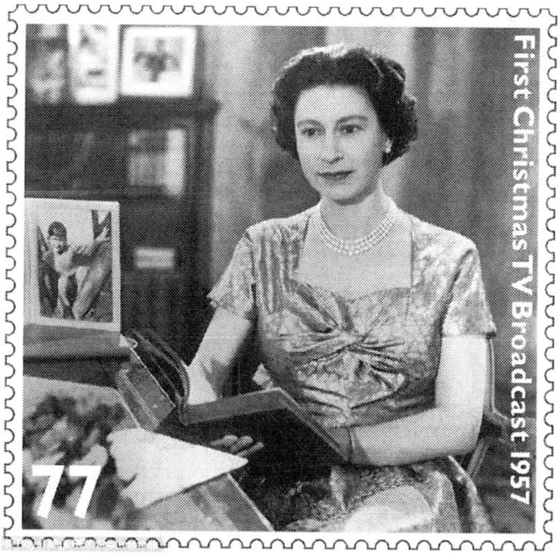
First Christmas TV Broadcast 1957
77

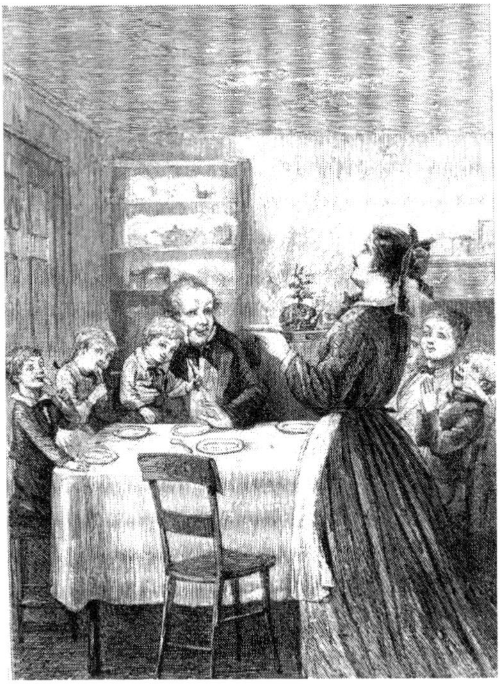

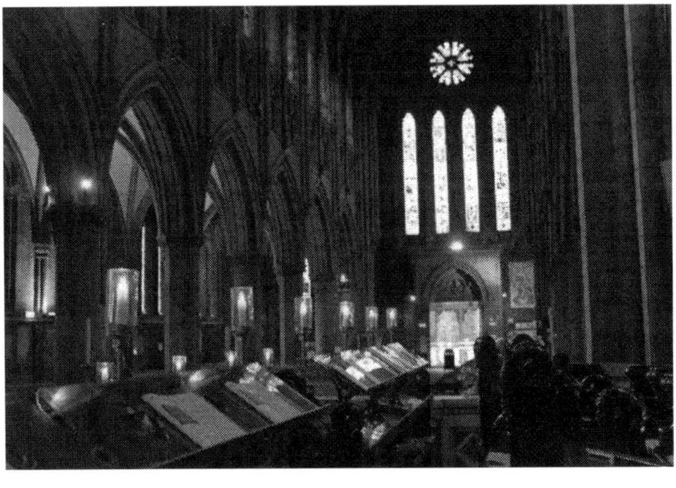

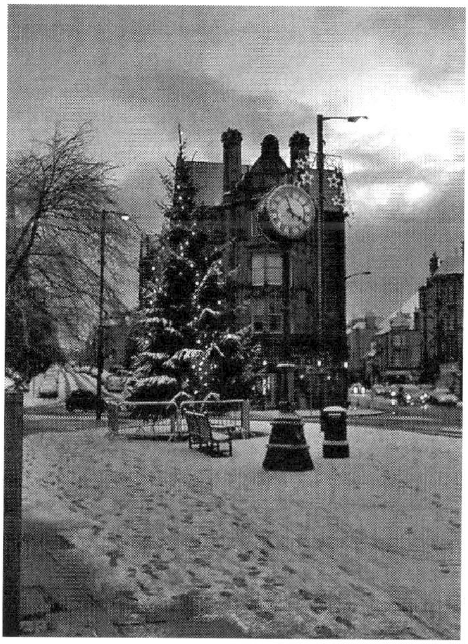

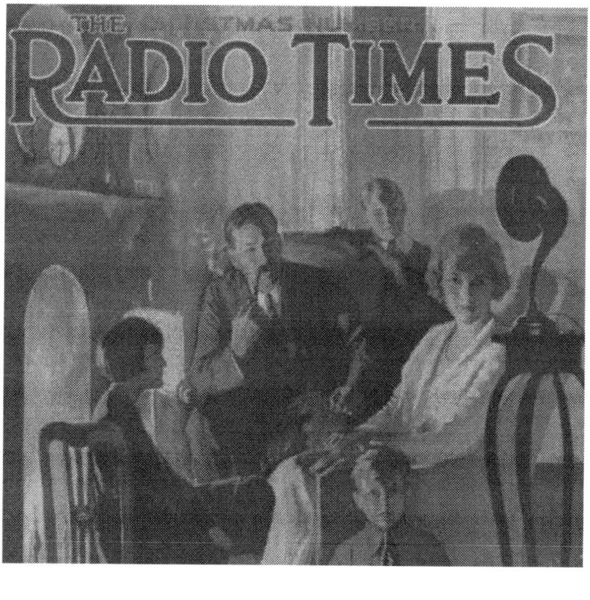
THE
RADIO TIMES

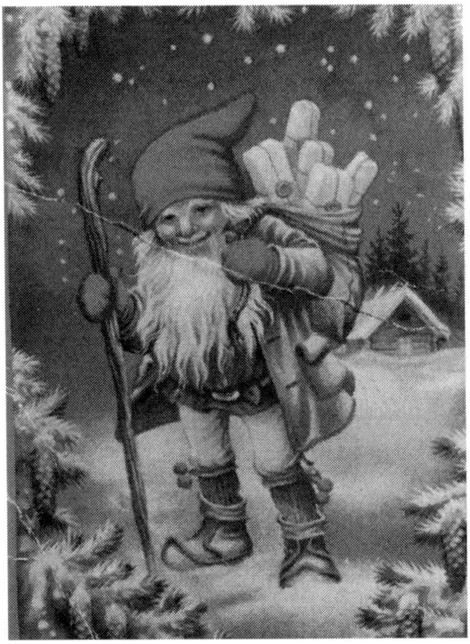

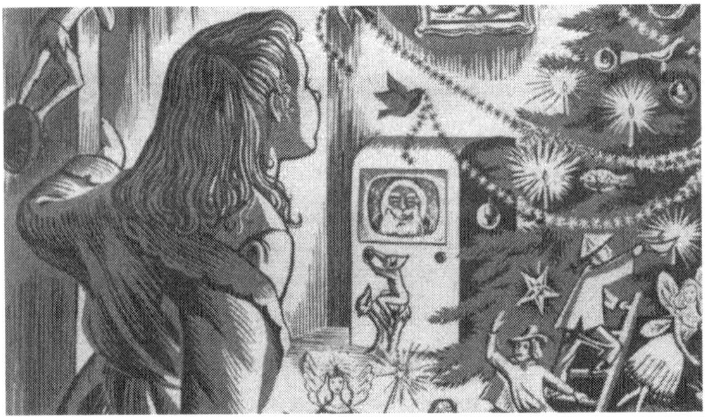

GORDON STOTT
Q.C.'s Diary
1954–1960
GORDON STOTT
Lord Advocate's Diary
1961–1966
GORDON STOTT
Judge's
1967–1973

WENT DOWN A SLIDE ON CORNHILL, TWENTY TIMES, IN HONOR OF ITS BEING CHRISTMAS-EVE.

Television Edition
RADIO TIMES
The Christmas Sound and Television Programmes
Christmas Day broadcast by His Majesty The King
3d

A Happy Christmas

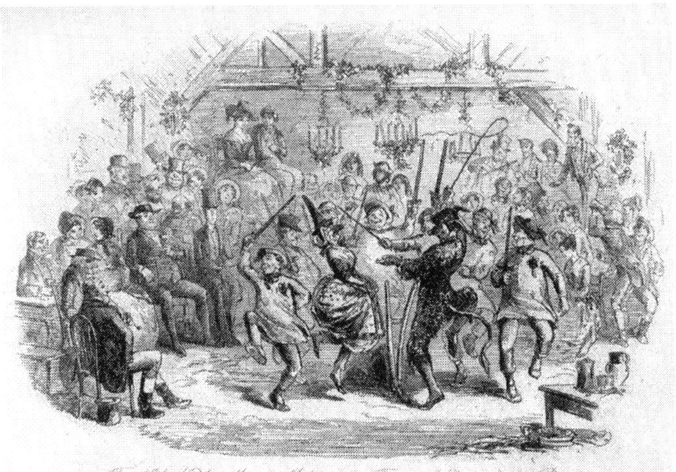

Twelfth Night Merry Making in Farmer Shakeshaft's Barn

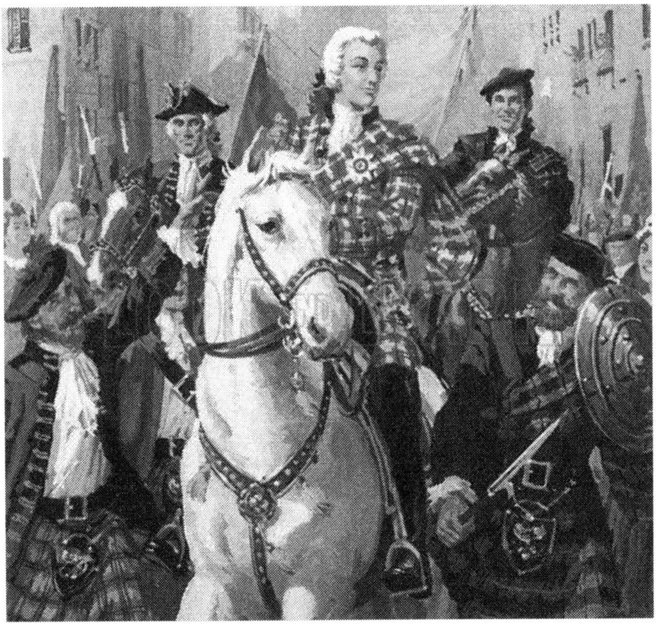

The Twelve Days of Christmas

The First Day of Christmas - Christmas Day

1971 Oxgangs Merry Christmas everyone. We still got our Christmas stockings from Mum but now that we're all getting slightly older they weren't at the foot of our beds this year but were still great as usual with lots of dinky wee pressies. Being Christmas Day we had a fancier brekkie than normal including fried bacon. The new telly was on in the background with some cartoons on 'Aspel's Christmas Crackers' followed by the 'Family Service'. We all then headed out to Corstorphine to the Harp Hotel. The morning was set fair dry and crisp but Oxgangs was as quiet as the proverbial church mouse as all the other families were either at home or away to relatives, however Corstorphine itself was a wee bit busier. I'm not quite sure why we've chosen the Harp Hotel as it's a bit awkward to get to from Oxgangs. I guess it's because it's got a good reputation and it's within our budget. It's not quite the same as the traditional Christmases we've all enjoyed at Joan's since I was born; however it was pretty good but I think we all may return to normality next year as long as we all give Joan a hand. Although the waitresses are lovely, going out to dinner is a bit more formal and not so relaxed - and it's kind of odd to be celebrating with strangers in the same room - still it gave Joan a wee break. We all went back to Porty to Joan and Darby's for the afternoon. The first part of 'Top of the Pops 71' was on - out of all the hits featured T Rex's 'Hot Love' was my favourite - *'She's faster than most And she lives on the coast'.* All the usual comforting fayre was on - 'The Queen'; 'Billy Smart's Circus' and then 'The Black and White Minstrel Show' - all relaxing stuff by way of background as we tucked in to a John West salmon tea and Joan's delicious home-made shortbread along with the usual buns. I didn't need any supper after three good feeds today. Darby gave us a lift home from Porty to Oxgangs. As usual as we sailed through an empty Arthurs Seat; there were hardly any cars on the road. Áine, Yohanan and I had a wee competition to count the number of lit Christmas trees we could see in the windows - aye auld habits die hard. Back home I was outside for a wee while talking away with Liz Fraser. Again another wee difference to the past when we always stayed within the bosom of the family home - aye we're all getting older. Back inside we all watched the 'Morecambe and Wise Show' which was enjoyable enough - Glenda Jackson was on doing a wee song and dance number. Funny enough the programme I enjoyed the most was the programme that concluded the day called 'The Countryman at Christmas' - a charming wee programme perfectly pitched to end the day. All and all a lovely day - and although different from previous years still a special one - we all enjoyed ourselves.

1972 Portobello Merry Christmas everyone. I opened up my Christmas stocking from Mum and there was some great stuff in there. In the morning I went out to St Mary's Church at Dalkeith for the Christmas morning service and also for Joan to put a wreath on Wee Nana's grave. Around mid-day Darby brought everyone down from Oxgangs. It was great for us all to be together once again for Christmas. You just can't beat Joan's on Christmas Day. Before lunch, Yohanan and I were out to Portobello Park to play football and then out the front at Durham Road. Lunch (Christmas Dinner) was brilliant. Roast turkey potatoes - I loved the two types of stuffing including sausage meat all followed by trifles and Arcari's ice cream then the Christmas pudding too. Whew! At the end of the day after a lovely tea including John West salmon sandwiches I travelled out to Oxgangs with everyone. I went up to see Fiona Blades. She's still going along to Charlotte Chapel which Paul and I have slipped away from going along to. I spoke to her about Moira Cameron about a possible date and she's going to speak to her for me which is great. Once back home to Porty I had a bath as I'm back to Thomas Graham's tomorrow. Boxing Day isn't a holiday in Scotland. I then sat by the fire watching 'Barefoot in the Park'.

1973 Portobello My second Christmas Day away from Oxgangs and on which I reflected upon later. After we exchanged presents Joan; Darby; Aunt Dottle and I travelled the seven miles along the quiet country back-roads from Portobello to Dalkeith Cemetery. Joan laid a beautiful home-made winter wreath on Pumpa and Wee Nana's graves. From Dalkeith once more on to quiet back-roads but this time traversing Midlothian to Oxgangs arriving just after mid-day. Mother gave me a Christmas stocking containing lots of thoughtful presents. For the second year we had our Christmas dinner at the Harp Hotel at Corstorphine; it was quite good but it's not the same as the usual family Christmas Day at Porty. To save on a taxi Darby made two separate trips back to Oxgangs. I was thinking how much I miss being with Áine and Yohanan at home;

I'm tempted to try and go back to stay at Oxgangs if I could but I guess the world has moved on and the clock can't be turned back.

1974 Portobello I lay in bed until about quarter to ten: I listened to the radio for most of the morning – Ed 'Stewpot' Stewart followed by Tony Blackburn. I got some nice presents which came as a surprise as I wasn't expecting anything now that I've hit the advanced age of eighteen – a Gillette razor; lots of Brut; Hai Karate and sweets, socks and underwear. After a marvellous Christmas dinner I watched the television. 'True Grit' was on. Yohanan; Áine; Mum; and John stayed until half past eleven at night watching 'The Bridge on the River Kwai'.

1975 Portobello I was up at about 9.30 am. After breakfast I sort of mucked about the house. The Oxgangs crowd arrived and Aunt Dottle's camera started whirring. It was quite a good day with quite a few laughs. Áine, Yohanan and I played records, mucked about with the dog and then settled back to watch television all evening. 'Morecambe and Wise' were okay. And then it was on to *Butch Cassidy and the Sundance Kid*. Bob Hope was on 'Parkinson' – he was really great.

1976 Portobello The car ignition was knackered but luckily for us the Customs Officer from the top of Durham Road temporarily fixed it for us. I picked up my sister at Oxgangs in the Triumph Spitfire. We had the usual super Christmas dinner courtesy of Joan. In the early afternoon I put the soft-top down and drove Áine and Yohanan out to Margaret's to see the Ross family at Henderson Row. With us having three in the car en-route we were keeping our fingers crossed we saw no policemen on the road but they both sat low in the passenger seat: actually good fun on Christmas Day. We headed back down to Porty – what a laugh! The family all gathered around the Halinavision projector to enjoy Aunt Dottle's film-show featuring some of her cine-films including a family Christmas from 1967 when we were all young with the best part Dad cursing in the kitchen, although there was no sound. We also watched films of Joan, Darby and Aunt Dottle at the Dublin Show as well as some of my races from Meadowbank. A lovely family late afternoon with lots of quips, repartee and laughs – a very lovely family occasion.

1977 Portobello I arose on Christmas morning at nine o'clock. The weather set fair - dry and sunny. I hoovered the house - its annual hoover before swinging round by Oxgangs to collect the family too. Z. kept us waiting for an hour. As ever and despite pushing 70, Joan served up a wonderful Christmas dinner for all the family. There was a lot of fun at the dinner table with many laughs with Aunt Dottle's camera snapping away in the background. Yohanan and Z. left early - supposedly to collect a 'big' present from K.'s father. Meanwhile, John and I spent an enjoyable few hours through in the front room playing Monopoly. Great - I won. Afterwards Áine and I phoned Dad - I think and I very much hope he's had as lovely a day us. I drove Mum; John and Áine back to Oxgangs and spent the evening watching the very excellent *Young Winston* - what an inspirational life - so very motivating making me want to do something with my own life too. But what a remarkable young man and guy. Z. and Yohanan dropped by later, Yohanan with his BIG pressie - a bottle of Brut! I dropped them off at their Marchmont flat and looked in for a coffee. I sat up late into the early morning of Boxing Day watching Bogie in *The Big Sleep*.

1978 Portobello Happy Christmas. I worked all morning giving 45 Durham Road its annual tidy up hoovering 'The Old Curiosity Shop'. Lunch was again fabulous. I over-indulged having a massive helping. My sister Áine and I bought some petrol at Crewe Toll - it's not often you find somewhere open in Edinburgh on Christmas Day. Come five o'clock we settled back by the fire with some tea and Christmas cake. In the evening I picked up Mum, John; and Áine and we went out to 6 Wester Coates Gardens to a Christmas party at Ronnie Browne's (of The Corries fame) - it was very quiet. I played some darts with Maurice (Browne) and later on Ronnie was able to show me the video of my race earlier in the summer for Great Britain against East Germany. I was ridiculously far down on Beyer and Straub with 250 metres to go. I stayed overnight at Oxgangs.

1980 Portobello (9.30 am) The snow came tumbling down - well, for fully five minutes; I know that, because I got caught out in it whilst out taking some exercise in preparation for the gluttony ahead. Around mid-day Mum; John; Yohanan; Áine; and her boyfriend Neil McGilvray arrived - it was smashing to see them all. I was delighted with my family present - a watch. I didn't think it would arrive before Christmas. It's absolutely beautiful - I'm so pleased with it. Joan prepared a wonderful dinner which I more than did justice to. A very lazy afternoon watching some old family home movies on Aunt Dottle's Halinavision. With no Darby anymore and no car, the Oxgangs crew managed to get an SMT green country bus at Milton Road West up to Edinburgh. By next year, if I graduate and secure a good job I might be able to treat myself to an MGB GT and therefore could squeeze one or two of them into that.

1981 The Northlands Happy Christmas. I was so excited when I awoke after a fitful night's sleep – the combination of yesterday's long train journey from Edinburgh and sleeping in a different bed. But it was so delightful because Martha and I had chosen to surprise each other with Christmas stockings and they really were surprises to both of us. I received many much-wanted pressies – a yellow tie; a golf glove; as well as a bag of gold. Later in the morning I joined all the Humphreys family to open presents. Bruce thoughtfully gave me a magnetic travel chess set whilst Wyvis and wife gave me thick socks and chocolates and then there was a new diary plus a record from Martha so along with a copy of the new Douglas Bader biography from Mum I did incredibly well. I went out for an hour's run across the fields and along the quiet country road to Strathpeffer. I was shocked at just how shockingly cold the Highland weather was. It was a very unusual dry cold so much so my hands were literally frozen and icicles had formed inside my nose – quite unbelievable. Wyvis's wifey served up a Christmas meal of salmon; turkey and the trimmings all followed by plum pudding; brandy butter and cream before I staggered away and slept for an hour. It was so very pleasant relaxing in the sitting room by an open log fire with the television on in the background and the gentle mulling sounds of the family and others talking happily away in the background. Martha and I retired to bed just before the midnight hour struck out. What a pity we'll have to await a whole year before Christmas Day comes back around once again.

1982 Portobello A Merry Merry Christmas. I was up at 6.00 am to excitedly see my Christmas stocking – small pleasures at both its appearance but also feeling the little wrapped gifts contained inside. And thereafter to carefully and lovingly take out and open each wrapped little item. Martha had been so thoughtful and made such a lovely job of the stocking. There was an (Steve) Ovett hooded running top; some books including Alan Massie's 'The Last Peacock' and Gray's 'Lanark'; a new diary and lots of other little serendipities – absolutely smashing getting Christmas Day off to a lovely start. Whereas, poor Mum said she'd not received a stocking since she was nineteen years old back in 1954. And how much she would still enjoy one. Which seems a shame. My sister didn't receive one either but Yohanan did courtesy of Mrs G. (X.'s mother). I spent part of the morning helping with the preparation of the meal as well as taking some pre-Christmas lunch exercise. As on the occasion of every Christmas Day past I tucked in. Spieler (Áine's future husband) was along and fitted in rather well. During the afternoon I entertained him and Mum through in the front room reading out extracts from 'The Paris Journal' (a holiday diary). Two telephone calls: one from Yohanan mid-morning including his two wee boys Kirk and Kent which was rather nice. I enjoyed his tale about playing Santa Claus last night and them seeing him out the window approaching the house from a distance and them immediately scampering off to bed so that they were good boys and that Santa would therefore have no excuse not to visit them. Darling Martha phoned in the afternoon just as the dog went missing. She wasn't feeling well but having fun and thinking affectionately of Samuel. Shortly after tea we set off for Oxgangs. I wanted to arrive early to allow me to pop down to Yohanan and K.'s for an hour. Their house was loud and noisy and in its way rather nice. And then back to watch a centenary celebration of James Joyce. Late to bed after staying up to watch a ghost story for Christmas Charles Dickens' *'The Signalman'* – Mum and I enjoy our traditional annual festive such fayre. Another Christmas comes and goes. The passing of the years.

1983 Portobello I hope it's not a sign of getting old but I felt slightly flat this Christmas morning. Anyway A Merry Christmas. I've put the light on and I'm opening my stocking and presents despite it only being ten minutes to six in the morning – *Robert Kennedy and his Times* by Arthur Schlesinger Jr.; a wine decanter; a John Kennedy memoir – *Johnny We Hardly Knew You* by O'Donnell; Powers; and McCarthy; a shirt; underwear; socks and jeans; a handkerchief; wee diary; and chocolates – all very nice. After breakfast a repeat of yesterday's housework. Mum and John arrived at mid-day. A quieter Christmas than usual when I consider the 1960s when there were four generations of the family around the dining table – quiet, but nice. Three telephone calls – from Yohanan; Áine and also from Martha in the Highlands. After tea

Mum; John and I left for Oxgangs. A long wait at a windy York Place for a 16 bus. Changed days again from the 1960s when we were all snug in the back of Darby's Ford Zephyr car travelling back home to Oxgangs as a family when we were just young kids. A quiet evening in with us enjoying 'All Creatures Great and Small'. Through in my old Oxgangs bedroom I read myself to sleep.

1984 Portobello Another nice Christmas Day spent at Joan's. At five o'clock whilst half-dozing on an armchair in the corner I watched Joan snoozing too, consciously aware that this is a good family Christmas day making myself fully appreciate the moment. We've recorded the day as Spieler videoed dinner, capturing some nice moments, although poor Aunt Dottie leapt out of the room after seeing herself on screen. Poor thing seeing herself looking pink, puffy and beady-eyed. It was just too much for her. I think we all take something out of seeing ourselves on screen. I'm terribly aware of my image too not to mention my inane conversation and wit - my dreadful speech and hesitant delivery. Poor appearance too. I should really work on my self-representational skills particularly my delivery with a view to ridding myself of my hesitations. Then there's my accent. And the lack of depth and originality in my utterings too. My voice is too high-pitched etc, etc. I'm surprised on reflection that I too didn't run out of the room! One piece of wit was immortalised – Joan to Mum – that teasing John could be done if only she were nice to him. As for the day itself it kicked off with a visit to the Paki's in Porty followed by coffee at Áine and Spieler's. Housework. A lovely lunch. Joan had made a grand job of it all. And she paced herself too, indeed over the whole festive holiday period. Late afternoon Martha phoned. I'm missing her and very much looking forward to seeing her again on her return from the Highlands. At eight o'clock Spieler drove us home to Oxgangs. I felt I'd have liked to have stayed down at Joan's this evening easing her out of Christmas. It must surely be an anti-climax for her after all the hard work and preparation she puts in to make Christmas Day so very special. I looked in to see Yohanan and Z. for a wee bit before Yohanan joined the family for supper.

1985 Powderhall/Portobello As we older people say 'Yes I had a rather quiet Christmas Day but very pleasant too.' I fell out of bed and did a little exercise up at Arthurs Seat but my cold is still hanging around. As a chap remarked to me at the pond 'It's mild.'

A light breakfast at Joan's then a bath back at the flat. Then a drive through a quiet Edinburgh in the Austin Allegro to collect Mum and John at Oxgangs. Yohanan's up to his tricks again driving Julie's car about and come three o'clock vanishing for the day. I gave Joan a hand with the lunch – the stuffing was cold and had to be quickly re-heated in a pot at the last minute – similarly the sausages and peas too. Aunt Dottle was useless. However a very nice Christmas dinner. John was quiet but the rest of us were chatting away. A few of us spent much of the afternoon through in the lovely surroundings of the front room. The road outside was quiet but an occasional person walked by taking in the Christmas air and spirit. I've enjoyed many decades at Christmas in this room going back to the late 1950s and early 1960s when the menfolk (Dad, Darby; and Pumpa) sat in here with their cigars; cigarettes; and pipe-smoke. I'm very pleased with Mum and John's present – 'The Oxford Companion to English Literature'. I received some socks from Aunt Dottle and a book token from my sister Áine. Yohanan has given me the Galliane shirt he'd bought for himself. Joan gave me an early oil painting she'd painted back in the day: it's a still life with bottles on a tables. It's classy and I'm pleased with it. Martha didn't telephone which was slightly surprising. But then I didn't contact her either. Ce la vie. We all looked into Áine and Spieler's for an hour. They had been working today for a few hours in her father-in-law Drew's restaurant in Portobello High Street – his latest venture. In the evening high winds and rain. I enjoyed the excellent *Absence of Malice* with some superb acting by Paul Newman. A very well structured and written film. I had no idea how it might end – great stuff. I drove back to the flat going to bed around 2.00 am after listening to some late night music.

1986 Oxgangs (1.00 am) Funny looking out the window and thinking it's now Christmas Day and yet I neither feel excited nor very special at all. And yet years ago when we were kids it was THE BIG DAY IN THE YEAR. This must be the first Christmas Eve I've spent at Oxgangs since, oh, 1971. Anyway on a more positive note I've pasted the very lovely Christmas card of a girl asleep on an old armchair next to a bright open fire. She's underneath a Christmas tree festooned with decorations whilst a fairy floats just above her. 'Christmas Dreams by the Fireside' (Anonymous). I love the colours – the card is a real beaut.

Later I didn't awake until around ten o'clock and somehow managed to take myself off for a run. It was lovely out – mild and sunny, perhaps the best day of the winter. There were two people out enjoying an unofficial round of golf high up on the Braid Hills and several other people out and about for a Christmas morning walk. It was actually so mild I could have got away with just a T-shirt and shorts. Down at Porty, Joan made a good job of our meal - remarkable really at her age (79). Several times she jocularly mentioned how by next year I might be able to host it at my recently purchased flat at Plewlands Terrace. That would be just fine and dandy by me. It would be a lovely way to help christen it and in her 80th year give Joan a very well-earned break. Something to very much look forward to. Throughout the day I occasionally observed Joan and reflected on how very good she was. Very sweet with none of the barbed remarks that she can sometimes come out with. In particular her demeanour towards me was in contrast with a slight coolness on my two previous visitations. Mother reckons that Aunt Dottle has changed somewhat after her spell in hospital. That she's become much more forthright – more opinionated – even quite bolshy. I'm delighted to hear it. She's also lost 12 lbs in weight – I sincerely hope she keeps it up – or should that be off – ah, the vagaries of the English language. I was glad that Áine and Spieler managed to remain for at least a part of the meal before heading off. Joan has painted a delightful Christmas card for Caomhog; it's a wee gem. In the evening Lee (clearly glad to escape from the house and family home) looked down to visit Yohanan and Audrey. It was a funny sort of an evening. Yohanan was very good – very hospitable - whereas his partner was okay but every now and then firing out some low level missiles - some waspish, sharpish comments. To be honest I found her to be a bit of a pain in the arse. As Mother also reiterated later on. I left at 10.30 pm. Lee arrived to become more sloshed. I thought about Martha once or twice today. I could have telephoned her on one or two occasions from Yohanan's but my instinct told me, no.

inverness christmas day 1986 dear samuel.. too lazy to use upper case I'm afraid..christmas really is just quite awful...the same old thing of eating too much, not drinking enough, arguing to heatedly and all around me snoring far too loud...it's been nice, in a familiar sort of way..too predictable to be exciting or terribly enjoyable...so the prospect of a new year in the highland capital is not one to relish..so I am keeping my fingers crossed we shall have no more snow, the slocht summit will stay open and I shall make it to Edinburgh for new year...I will telephone when I arrive..and will I think be staying at my brother's flat for at least some of the time....I'm not sure what is happening at Hogmanay...I have semi arranged to see anne and john...probably at bill walker's...I don't imagine it would be a very good idea to arrive (or leave) there with you...I mean for the sake of your thing with elfin...I'm sure we can sort something out...can we (no question marks on this machine...) I know I would like to see you very much...a trifle foolish no doubt but, well foolish no doubt but, well foolishness seems to be one of my strengths so I am confident I can suffer on Sunday very much..a pity I find I am emotionally and otherwise articulate only when partially (or completely) drunk but that I am afraid seems to be my lot...self-induced or fatalistic I am not sure...any way I look forward to seeing you again very much..and hope you will be able to fill me in on the whys and wherefores of the evaporation of my golf lessons, tea in jenners etc!

much love amelia xxxxxxxx

1988 Morningside Well, now that I'm a property owner and as prompted by Joan two years ago, the Laird o' Plewlands hosted his second Morningside Christmas and the family got some pleasure and enjoyment out of the day. The lunch went fine – I only managed to burn four roast potatoes. After half an hour I ushered Joan out of the kitchen – I wanted to keep her out of the way. The family were up to high-doe about Aunt Dottle's present – would she like them? My poor sister couldn't take it and disappeared to the kitchen. After everyone had left, Mother and John stayed on and enjoyed themselves the more so for being ensconced in the sitting room with the gas fire burning brightly in the Victorian-style fireplace. Mother is fine once she dismantles the guard's van of the train dropping the bitterness and begins to laugh out aloud moving away from deriding others showing herself in a better light to others. As the day progressed Audrey enjoyed herself feeling a part of the family. Spieler blends in well laughing and remaining in a world of his own engrossed in magazines. John (tearful at the beginning?) similar to Spieler enjoying the day the longer it went. Caomhog is a delight. For a while she slept through in the small bedroom. I begin to understand why Joan and Darby would have liked to have adopted me when I was young. When I see her I feel I could easily move on to the role of being a parent.

1989 The Northlands (3.45 pm) Dinner is about to be served – yahoo! Wyvis's wife kindly left me a Christmas stocking full of useful little serendipities – golf balls; deodorant; socks etc. They (Wyvis and Wife) also gave me a cravat and a record token: the latter most acceptable as there's around thirty albums that I'm keen to buy just now much of it garnered from Q Magazine. We didn't get to sleep until around 3.00 am this morning and we were up by 9.00 am. Fortunately young Gavin (Martha's youngest brother) didn't get up until later to inspect Santa's good-work. A Buck's Fizz breakfast including bacon; mushrooms; eggs; and toast. Outside it's wet and damp and windy and dusk has fallen. I'd gone out for a run at lunchtime on the surrounding country roads and fields and got soaked. Still, it's left me feeling good with a grand appetite. Wyvis's wife's mother is here; she is down about her husband who is dying in hospital in Inverness. I tried to imagine how I might feel if after a life-time together it was Martha. I telephoned Dad and young Roddy – they were having Chinese.

Later A lovely Christmas dinner and once more in the conservatory. Wyvis's wife's mother became quite chatty – drank a bit – and seemed to enjoy herself. I telephoned Porty and spoke to Áine; Mum; Aunt Dottle and Joan who were all sat by a roaring fire enjoying *Crocodile Dundee* and then a Miss Marple which of course I couldn't follow.

1990 Morningside Well the Laird o' West Mill hosted his first Christmas here in Colinton. Martha was in the northlands once again so it was lovely to have my family over to stay for our country Christmas in the city. The day flew by. At 10.00 am I drove down from Colinton to Porty to collect Joan and Aunt Dottle. En-route I passed Robin Morris; Henry and A.N. Other out running through the Hermitage of Braid. Once back to Colinton it was back to the kitchen and all go. Yohanan was in with me but his mood altered and varied the more he drank – from morose to hilarity, etc. So including myself there were half a dozen of us sitting down for dinner – Mum and John; Joan and Aunt Dottle; Yohanan and me.

1993 Colinton A white Christmas with snow on the ground here at Colinton and also one or two small flurries. Around eight o'clock Martha's nephews Loki and Thor (down from Ullapool) opened their stockings before going back to bed. Reflecting on Christmas at that moment I thought how commercial and distasteful it's become and the obscenity of being surrounded by dozens of presents opened then casually tossed aside and the still to be opened presents around the tree – less is most definitely more. Martha, her sister and I sat in the sitting room opening our pressies afterwards. Come eleven o'clock a Buck's Fizz breakfast with a fry up. I seconded John to chauffeuring duties putting the family off until two o'clock. I worked solidly in the dining room and by the time Martha had finished the table it looked really rather lovely especially when the clock struck four o'clock in the afternoon and we lit the candles. Fourteen seats around the table – quite amazing really. A real extended family Christmas. Mother; John; Joan and Aunt Dottle arrived early at twenty to two; Martha, her sister and I were still in our bedclothes as we hadn't bothered getting changed whilst we'd pushed on with the preparations. As we belted around it was like the Le Piat D'or advert. John apologised for arriving early but it was common knowledge who had caused it! Despite so many people I thought the dynamics didn't really work and the mood was surprisingly subdued with the only laughs coming when I was showing people to their seats. Occasional laughs emanated from Yohanan through in the kitchen. But Joan was very subdued – she has a cold and was happy to leave early with Yohanan at seven o'clock. Sinéadte was actually very good trying to get people talking. Áine insisted on giving a hand to help clean up afterwards. The two sets of kids Loki and Thor and Caomhog and Lulu played well together. Aunt Dottle was, well Aunt Dottle. As always John didn't interact socially but was very good helping to entertain the kids. Mother sat around like Lady Muck not even getting up to see Joan off or offering a helping hand. In the evening people were still running around at the back of her; Martha and her sister worked like Trojans all the day long. In the evening a few of us relaxed in including Mum and John – I enjoy seeing them relaxed in and being able to offer and share in our good fortune by sharing our large extended cottage and garden grounds – our wee bit of paradise – our countryside in the city. Watching *'Field of Dreams'* I'd forgotten just what a good film it is with a big message in there. As he (Kevin Costner) threw the ball I recalled the day when Dad, Yohanan, Roddy and I did the same with a rugby ball down at Meggetland. It's now the second year since Dad isn't around to enjoy Christmas so it was good that he received a small passing thought on this most special day in the calendar year.

1995 Colinton Only three hours of sleep before wee Atticus (age 19 months) was up. I was surprised at the vigour with which he opened the small parcels in his little stocking managing each and every item. There was a harmonica; a flat village for his cars; chocolate coins; an apple and an orange (which he proceeded to eat); a box of plastic food and grocery items and other little serendipities. Martha kindly gave me an extra few hours before calling me down to our farmhouse-kitchen for a large traditional Christmas Day breakfast. Atticus and I drove down to Stenhouse Gardens North to Mother's. The light dusting of snow out in Edinburgh was just enough to give us all the pleasure of a White Christmas but of course with none of the inconvenience of it. Whereas in the northlands and out on the Isles they've experienced their worst snow for forty years. It was very pleasant down at Mum's with John helping Atticus to open their large present to him of a desk; Mother looked as if she was taking some good photographs of the scene. All in all a very positive hour spent together. Later on Joan said that Mother had complained that Yohanan and Sinéadte were out and about visiting but not round to see her. I struggled to eat my pheasant Christmas lunch but still did it full justice. Martha had made a lovely job of cooking it. Thereafter a quiet Christmas afternoon with one or two telephone calls. Martha's dad Wyvis is in bed with a poisoned foot. There was a gargantuan feast of family and friends presents under the tree for Atticus including books; dressing gown and slippers; a fire engine; anorak; vests; Duplo; a suit dungarees and shirt. Late on I sat up alone surprisingly enjoying 'Indecent Proposal'.

The Second Day of Christmas
Boxing Day

1971 Oxgangs The good weather continues - crisp and cold but sunny allowing a bunch of us to enjoy a very good game of football. Brilliant fun and it was just great to be able to get outside on Boxing Day and to be able to run around. I had another game of footie later on but across at the playground toward dusk under the street lights. Unfortunately Stephen Westbrook kept spoiling for a fight during the game and picked a fight with me; I ended up kicking him in. I hated the whole thing and it's not like me to get involved in that way - probably the only fight I've had all year; I would rather run a mile than get involved. Anyway it all started off in front of everyone and I just had to feign some chutzpah and get on with it. No doubt everything will return to normality. Afterwards and to make things worse I ended up having a bad fall on to the concrete late on in the game - flipping OUCH. I'm being hit from all sides. I came back to 6/2 and settled down to watch 'High Society' on the new telly. It was brilliant - a great film with some lovely tracks. Just thinking of old Louie Armstrong singing the soundtrack brings a smile to my face. I'm planning to go out for a wee run with Paul later on at 7.00 pm tonight.

1972 Portobello With yesterday being Christmas Day it was slightly strange going back to work at Thomas Graham's this morning. It's completely different to all my previous Boxing Days when I've been at school and therefore on holiday – welcome to the grown up world of work. But it meant for a slightly more relaxed day at work and it was quieter too. I went along to Morningside at lunchtime and it was quiet there too; quite a few of the shops were closed but not the chip shop. In the evening I went up to Meadowbank Sports Centre to train. We trained indoors with me running some back to back 100s in the concourse area underneath the stand. I trained with Robin Morris and we did 3 x 6 x 100 metres at three-quarters speed. Once back home to Porty I was thinking about the lovely Moira Cameron as I had at various times during the day; it would be great to go out with her. I'm watching Alf Garnett on the telly in 'Till Death Us Depart'. It's a Christmas special.

1973 Boxing Day (Holiday except in Scotland) Portobello Grandma Joan wasn't up to speed with Graham's ways. It was quite funny; Joan thought I was still on holiday today and didn't awaken me. I didn't get up until ten o'clock. I phoned Paul and we decided to go to see 'Magnum Force' with Chris Cole. The film was good and a strong follow up to 'Dirty Harry'. Dr Motley's signed me off work till next Thursday. I ended up staying at Oxgangs tonight so quickly ran down to the phone-box at Colinton Mains to let Darby know. 'The Two Ronnies' were very funny.

1977 Portobello Today will be the worst day of my cold. Apart from a quick short excursion down to Nan's at Southfield Place to pick up some milk and rolls Darby and I stayed in all morning playing 'Monopoly'. After lunch we resumed playing – back to the board with a determined doggedness to win, which I did: it was funny at one stage when Darby lost his temper - I had to suppress my laughter. Later on we sat up watching *The Dirty Dozen*.

1980 Portobello A lovely crisp morning out. I took the dog for a walk and en-route stopped by the telephone box outside Swann's Newsagent's and called Dad: he was delighted to hear from me. Later I made a mass clearance of my bedroom throwing out bagfuls of stuff and re-arranged the furniture too - tiring but I felt in need of a change - symptomatic of course of my life just now. In the evening I dressed up and joined the Ross's for dinner at 6 Henderson Row: a very pleasant evening later playing charades into the night: I stayed downstairs not getting to bed until 3.30 am

1981 The Northlands Boxing Day It didn't really feel like a Saturday; as Martha remarked, the quietest Saturday of the year. I was out early on the big hill: as usual I put down on paper far too much; you quickly forget how hard going it is. Anyway that over I could afford to relax for a bit sitting around reading the biography 'Bobby Fischer Profile of a Prodigy' by Frank Brady which I'm enjoying interspersed with the odd game of 'Blockade'. Around three o'clock Martha and I went out for a pleasant walk toward Strathpeffer sticking to the frozen farm paths which had a light covering of powdered snow. A fresh and crisp Boxing Day walk with a cold breeze on the return. Once back we treated ourselves to a couple of the chocolate delicacies from her stocking. And come the evening a lovely turkey fricassee with plenty of greens to accompany it. The two of us spent the evening by the coal fire up at Home Comfort Farm babysitting for Robbie and Helen. Despite the intermittent power cuts we watched 'The 39 Steps' and stayed up until midnight. Back to Northlands, naughty couples abounded.

1982 Oxgangs At lunchtime I went out for a heavyweight run over the Pentland Hills; I was out for over an hour. It was hard going on the climb up the slopes but on reaching the peaks it was heaven to just glide along the hill tops - Torphichen to Swanston and then on to Hillend. A solitary run through the countryside feeling completely at one with myself. Staying at Oxgangs over the holiday period opens up the opportunity for some delightful runs. I spent the rest of the day at Lee's. Good fun. We sat and blethered away for several hours. Julie (his mum) kindly gave me a bowl of homemade soup as well as a glass of orange brandy. Later on his father, Big Lee, arrived so we had a very humorous few hours with Big

Lee perhaps being a little bit hard on Roy who was left reeling by his wit especially when he was taking the piss out of poor Roy's bald head. On a positive note however he did serve us all up a meal. Later on Martha telephoned. She's missing me.

1983 Oxgangs I spent much of Boxing Day through at the Rigbys. They appreciated Joan's home-made sweets – marzipan walnuts; fudge; peppermint creams, etc. that I'd brought over for them. I telephoned Joan; read; eat; did a little bit of exercise across in the City Hospital on a very lovely and beautiful morning out – a crisp white frost with the sun high in a crystal clear blue sky above Hillend. I did some bounding and then some sprints on the cricket pitch. There was a lovely family grouping out with their dog for a Boxing Day walk who wished me a cheery good morning. Martha called. Not so warm. Funny old world isn't it. I spent the evening with Lee watching telly and talking till late into the early morning.

1984 Oxgangs I went out to run off my Christmas lunch – a bit gingerly to begin with because of some recent problems with my leg but once I got to Braidburn Valley onward I began to flow along with it turning into a lovely run on a cracking morning – crisp, cold and rather beautiful out buoyed by the good cheer of a few people out, mainly dog-walkers. A late breakfast at mid-day – a brunch I suppose with Áine and Spieler; Yohanan meanwhile looked by for ten minutes. I spent the afternoon with Lee. He was regaling us (Yohanan briefly) with his adventures over the festive period drinking heavily including a car going over his ankle. Blimey! Lee and I chatted intermittently but I also enjoyed getting stuck in to Julia's (Lee's mother) copy of Jimmy Boyle's *'The Pain of Confinement'*. A very interesting and stimulating read. He now believes in and practices and says so very much that I agree with myself. By nine o'clock I'd read the first 100 pages. Mum and John rattled up a giant portion of steak pie and mash for me – very filling. Prior to my meal I'd telephoned Joan thinking Boxing Day must be a bit of an anti-climax for her. It was. I could tell by her voice. Outside the temperature has fallen dramatically. Jack Frost has already been out and about working his magic. Supper. Miss Marple – 'The Body in the Library'; Dave Allen and an hour of 'The Third Man' before hitting the sack. Unfortunately I'm back to work tomorrow to the Scottish Episcopal Church.

1986 Oxgangs I awoke at 8.00 am but it felt more like five o'clock. I rattled on Lee's window pane but no reply. I telephoned Yohanan's flat at Bruce Street Morningside. He was there. We met up for a Boxing Day round of golf on the Braid Hills - Yohanan; Lee; Raymond and me. But horror of horrors, Audrey was there. I couldn't believe it when she followed us all the way round - talk about the spectre at the feast. Brass necked and completely lacking in empathy. Anyway, despite her presence I enjoyed the game with Lee winning come the 17th hole with 11 Stableford points and the rest of us on 10. The weather wasn't nearly as good as yesterday but good for late December in the season of the year. A light lunch followed by a wee snooze. Mid-afternoon I ran a pleasing session at Arthurs Seat before looking into Joan's . Áine and Spieler were there. Joan was sitting down looking content but perhaps a little weary. She was enjoying watching Áine with Caomhog, perhaps bringing back memories of her being a mother herself, half a century before. I watched how Caomhog stared. I asked Áine if she wondered just what babies were thinking. Like me she had no idea. I also saw them later at Oxgangs. Back at the flat I did a little recording but I'd essentially looked back to watch Laurens van der Post being interviewed by Jonathon Stedall the same chap who made one of my very favourite series - 'Malcolm Muggeridge - Ancient and Modern'. I enjoyed it. But really it was only a taster. It was interesting to see a copy of his first book produced by the Woolfs (The Hogarth Press) - I have that very copy sitting by my side - 'In a Province' which I picked up at Sam Burns' Yard at Prestonpans. I admire van der Post for being not just an adventurer and philosopher but as a writer too. I don't think I really considered telephoning Martha in the Highlands whilst at Oxgangs but would have enjoyed hearing from her down here at the flat. So far I've not really written anything down but on Sunday evening who turned up at the front door but Amelia - I got quite a pleasant shock. We met later and somewhat apprehensively for a drink or six and got on rather well although I had verbal diarrhoea. She's in a bit of a depression. There was a telling comment of her long long journey from Bournemouth and of how she kept seeing all the couples in their cars driving northwards for Christmas. Also in retrospect was it not rather unusual that she'd turned up at the house out of the blue on the spur of the moment. After all, apart from her brother, she hadn't thus far visited any of her other friends. I think she must have been very low. In my drunken state

I told her she needed a good cuddle. I walked her back to her brother's flat in the Dean Village. She asked me to keep New Year free. I wonder though whether in the cold light of dawn and in the intervening period she might just decide to give any get-together a miss. For fun and out of interest I looked up my diary – six and a half years back to 1980 – incredible - to find out whatever happened between us. I was very depressed at the time; and for the lack of a better phrase our relationship just 'petered out'.

1988 Morningside 4:00 p.m. Over the years I've enjoyed reading jokes about unwanted Christmas presents. Today – Boxing Day – every time I glimpsed the golf book that Yohanan and Audrey gave me which probably cost them an extortionate £25? – I felt a pang knowing that I'll never read it and reflecting on what delights I might have bought after an afternoon of delight in a second hand bookshop perhaps picking up 3 or 4 serendipities for such an amount.

1989 The Northlands (4.45 pm) A lazy day. I drove into The Northlands for The Times and a couple of other newspapers. Patches of sunshine out and on the Strathpeffer Road some Boxing Day orienteers. I've just completed some short snappy runs. Robbie, Helen, Uberlegen and young Koch have just arrived. Where are they all going to sleep?

1993 Colinton Christmas Sunday There's been a little more snow. After lunch, once again I took the boys (Loki and Thor) sledging to the Merchants Golf Course. Much fun with some spectacular crashes. The best crash was undoubtedly a young boy who shot four feet up in the air vertically up a tree followed by a backward somersault. Martha and her sister arrived later to do some filming with my camera. Afterwards they both fell asleep early whilst I stayed up until 1.30 am watching a nice wee double bill – 'The Outlaw Josey Wales' followed by a 'Neil Diamond Christmas Special'. I've enjoyed the holiday break but the days have passed quickly. I'm now starting to look forward to the New Year with the wonderful prospect of our new baby in the spring; the exciting challenge of much cost-cutting and thinking of how I might make some more money; redistributing my time better; and of course just what is going to happen with Local Government Reorganisation; and also whether Martha should continue to work and much much else. 2.45 am The double bed is crowded out with Martha and the cats Biff and Fearty so I wandered upstairs to the single room.

1995 Colinton The big freeze continues unabated – minus 12 degrees centigrade and that was inside the garden hut at the foot of the garden! But a beautiful day with a clear sky sunshine and a fine winter landscape. Along with wee Atticus (19 months) we took Joan and Aunt Dottle for a wee outing down to East Lothian – very quiet out and about on the car run but a really wonderful outlook particularly coming back through the delightful small villages of Stenton and Gifford. Just before dusk fell Martha, Atticus and I went for a walk to Blackford Pond; it was frozen over. I was surprised to see the ducks still clambering for the bread we'd brought along thinking they would have been well fed today with all their earlier Boxing Day visitors. Áine and the girls (Caomhog and Lulu) dropped by with some presents for Atticus: Áine low.

The Third Day of Christmas
27th December

1971 Oxgangs We're getting a good crack of the whip with the fine weather this Christmas Holiday from school; it's not always been this good. Once again we got a bunch of us out for a game of football down at Colinton Mains Park. The postie arrived for the first time since Christmas Eve and it was a good one for us all as there was Christmas money from Dad. I got a fiver so went into town with Yohanan, Boo-Boo and Paul and bought myself a new parka - just what I need for the cauld winter mornings on my paper runs. We had a braw fun time in town ending up at Woolies café Princes Street once again and then getting some fun photies in the booth. In the evening I watched 'Carry On Cowboy'; I thought it was crap. I'm off to bed now. I'm fair enjoying my holidays.

1972 Portobello Big 6 foot 3 karate black-belt Ronnie Wisdom who's a bit of an enigma hit me at work today. He was just in one of his strange dour moods and suddenly lashed out. He came back later in the day and apologised. There was no reason for it really. He's come through to the office and Roy was being a bit witty with him and I was laughing and all of a sudden he just lashed out. I wasn't laughing at him - Roy's pretty funny at times. After work I headed out to Saughton and did a five mile run up to Craighouse and Slateford which I quite enjoyed as for once I was able to keep up with the pack. I came back to Portobello. I'm going to bed to dream about Moira Cameron who I know from Charlotte Chapel: she attends Mary Erskine's School.

1973 Portobello I didn't feel too good when I awoke this morning. I phoned Bill up. Yohanan got his new radio for Christmas. I travelled down to Waugh's Butcher's shop at lunchtime to meet Darby. In the afternoon we had our first day back at training; it was great to be able to train at this time rather than being stuck in at work. Later Paul and I beat Scott Brodie and the good badminton player Alan Bowes in a doubles take-on at table tennis. In the evening I stayed down and did some block-work with A. and her coach. I was talking with Fiona. I'd like to get off with her. Stuart Gillies gave me a lift home afterwards straight to the door – good lad.

1975 Portobello Having taken three days off to recover from the cold and with the prospect of the Phillips' Invitational Indoor 600 metres approaching I lay in bed until about ten thinking about this 600 metres time trial. I wandered up to Meadowbank. I ran well sitting on Norman Gregor and kicking past him on the final bend. It was a good time given the poor conditions; it was very windy and cold but at least it was dry.

1976 Portobello I ran a very hard session with Adrian Weatherhead at Meadowbank. In the evening Yohanan and I went out for a drink – we were kind of steamboats.

1977 Portobello I drove Joan out to Dalkeith Cemetery to lay a wreath on the graveyard of Wee Nana and Pumpa. It was a most beautiful morning out – sunny and dry with a very bright sun. But poor Darby awoke with a terrible cold: with his dreadful health, heaving heart and lungs and breathlessness it's the very last thing he could do with. He was croaking like a frog. From Dalkeith, Joan and I drove round by Oxgangs to hand in some dance tickets – fortunately Mum and John were in and we enjoyed some lovely ham sandwiches. Back at Portobello, Bill Walker phoned – would I run a time trial to help out one of the Pros in training for New Year? Which I did. Having been off with a cold I didn't run particularly well but it helped the Pro runner out, so fair enough. We had some Chinese food before watching 'The Corries on the Road' on the box and then onward to the dance around eleven o'clock. There was a spot of trouble when someone tried to move me from my seat but I stood my ground.

1980 6 Henderson Row/Portobello I got up around 10.30 am. The rest of the household was still asleep so I penned a thank you note to David; Frances and Lauren and slipped out the door. I bumped into Mr Cousins the Manpower lecturer – a nice chap but someone who's marking I'm at complete odds with. I gave Dad a ring; he's leaving for London this afternoon and then onward to Belgium. I worked away on Accounts today as well as pottering around sorting out a few cassettes. An evening in front of the box – a delightful play by Frederick Lonsdale was on called 'On Approval' – it was about two couples seeing if marriage was the bliss they thought it might be – the cast were excellent – Jeremy Brett; Penelope Keith; and Lindsay Duncan - very charming and quite beautiful.

1981 The Northlands I was out working quite hard on the short hill this morning. Once I got back to Northlands, Martha had been arguing with her father. The upshot is that we're to leave on the four o'clock train back to Edinburgh. However by lunchtime things were patched up, that is until Wyvis's wifey came out with an ill-considered remark to Martha. Her dad helped put things right. In the afternoon we travelled over to Muir of Ord to visit Martha's friend Nell and husband Donnchadh. They did Martha well – a pair of sheepskin slippers and a tartan shirt. The afternoon passed by reasonably well but with some of the conversation just a little stilted. A quiet relaxed evening in by the fire reading the Sunday newspapers with the television on in the background including the final of 'Mastermind'.

1982 Oxgangs Today it was SNOOKER SNOOKER and SNOOKER. At ten o'clock Lee and I went down to Demarco's Slateford Road and played until lunchtime with Lee winning 4-0. We ran for a number 4 bus and got back to Oxgangs for a good bit of lunch – toasted cheese, soup and biscuits. Margaret Elliot-Ross was in, well just leaving with John, to head out to Stobsmills House Gorebridge to look at the electrics. Lee, Yohanan and I went down the Angle Club (also owned by Bert Demarco) in Morningside and we played snooker all afternoon. Lee's father who's an ever present at the club came over and joined us for a final game. We all rather enjoyed ourselves. A lazy evening in watching 'Moonraker' with plenty of scran to eat. Martha had telephoned when I was out to say she isn't coming back before Friday (today's Monday) – she told me last week it would be by Thursday if not Wednesday...hmm.

1983 Oxgangs I did a little exercise but it was miserable out as was my cold. I spent much of the day with Lee talking until late-late. Food and a book. Earlier in the day Joan called me – the silly 'girl' had tried to paint the living room and with her heavy cold had ended up knackering herself. I went down straight away. I was a little concerned but didn't show it. I completed the job and gave both her and Aunt Dottle a slight ticking off. I met Martha at the bus station on her return from the Highlands and carried her bags home down to Dunedin Street. She was cool, irritable and unpleasant to me treating me disgracefully so I just left to spend the evening and night at Oxgangs. I was annoyed about it when I reflected on it all.

1984 Oxgangs I felt rather out of sorts today having to return to work to the Scottish Episcopal Church offices after the festive break. It felt quite different to returning after a weekend off. My feelings are perhaps influenced with a new job on the horizon (Community Recreation Officer Midlothian District Council). But Jackie was restless too. DLS (David Logan-Smith) was his incredible self once again informing Jackie that the UTP job is going to be scrapped and given over to Ivory & Sime to do in future yet he didn't even consider telling me. Yet another example of this man's failure to communicate with his staff. Is it bad manners, a lack of thought, a lack of intelligence or what? And yet he can also be a nice guy too. Later on I did a wee circuit at Meadowbank and a light track session too on a white frost covered running track. The overnight frost has been the heaviest of the winter and indeed it's been the coldest too. I spent the early evening down at Porty at Joan's . She was still working away on dolls for Martha and for Margaret Ross. Later on I walked down to Portobello to Áine and Spieler's: Mum and John were there. We lounged about watching the box including the second part of Miss Marple: *'The Body in the Library'* before poor Spieler gave us all a lift home after eleven o'clock.

1985 Oxgangs I was awoken at Mum's at a quarter to nine with the sound of the phone ringing – it was Joan to say that she had just had the gas-man out. There had been a leak in the pipe by the fire. She had Mr Prior from 41 Durham Road replete in his pyjamas up to switch the gas off. I took Mum and John down to Safeways for their messages before training on hard rutted ground at Holyrood Park, the result of an overnight frost. I was in town for an hour with nothing (books) taking my fancy. Oxgangs for tea (John's unusual combination of toasted cheese, bacon and egg) but very pleasant. Mum's going down with a cold whilst I've still a headache at the back of my head. A TV evening. A (Friday evening) drink in town. Home.

1989 Home Comfort Farm The Northlands (4.00 pm) I've just collected Doug (Martha's half-brother) from the hospital – Hoch (Martha's nephew) and her younger half-brother Gavin were along too. As for Gavin well the neologism (word) 'obnoxious' was clearly introduced with him in mind. Wyvis was back for lunch. He managed to run over and half kill a hen. Martha, her brother Robbie and young Koch are away to Ullapool. In the evening there were around seventeen in for supper – Martha's relation Rory (an actor) is a nice bloke and I enjoyed speaking with him.

1990 Colinton Well we were closer to a white Christmas than everybody perhaps realised. This morn there was between two and three inches of snow and a little more fell intermittently throughout the day. Biff and Fearty (the cats) royally entertained Yohanan and me; from the upstairs bathroom window we looked out on them dancing about and playing in the back garden chasing each other's tails and turning somersaults in the air. We'd wished we'd had a video camera handy to have captured the moment. Mentioning somersaults made me think how quickly the time has flown since those lazy summer July days when we played with water and eat alfresco in our back garden. Christmas then has come and gone. Last evening Martha telephoned from the Highlands enjoying an evening by the fireside. We meanwhile had a Chinese carry out whilst watching *Manon de Sources*. Wonderful stuff. I drove Mum, John and Yohanan home this morning. Mum said how very much they'd enjoyed themselves staying over at West Mill.

1993 Colinton Boxing Day Some general housework in the morning and then an hour or so in town looking at some of the Boxing Day Sales items. I bought an attractive golf-illustrated tin with socks inside for John D's upcoming birthday. I timed myself from the Caledonian Hotel car park area to West Mill Road – 13 minutes - so although we're far out on the fringes of the capital in the lea of the Pentland Hills that's not bad going to essentially the centre of town and a small price for living here in the countryside in the town. At three o'clock Martha; her sister and her boys Loki and Thor and I went for a walk along the Water of Leith and climbed up as far as the High Stables and then homeward bound. A winter full moon. The fields covered in snow. The horses with their winter coats on keeping perhaps a little of the cold at bay. It's cold. And still. The boys galloped and cavorted like wild horses. After all the scranning Martha's sister enjoyed the exercise.

The Moon is in the River

The moon is in the river

The snow on the path. Still.

Running home at dusk

Home. To West Mill.

The Fourth Day of Christmas

28th December

1971 Oxgangs This is turning in to a really enjoyable school holiday perhaps the best Christmas one ever and surprisingly good on the fitness front. First thing in the morning I went off for an enjoyable wee run along to Braidburn Valley. After breakfast we had another cracking game of football with me scoring a dozen goals - I'm a machine. At dinnertime a group of us all went for another wee tootle in to town - all that Christmas money jingling about in our pockets. In the evening we watched Steve McQueen in 'The Great Escape' - an absolutely fantastic film - a classic with McQueen as cool as anything. Although it finished at 9.15 pm a few of us went out afterwards for a wee while and hung about talking.

1974 Portobello I went up to Meadowbank to do my first training session after being off. It was pretty tough going. Bill Walker my athletics coach had to shout at me to finish it but I was glad that he did. I played table tennis in the afternoon. In the evening Aileen Gordon and I went along to see 'That'll Be The Day'. It was quite good. It was raining when we came out. We couldn't get any coffee as all the places were closed so I just saw her on to her bus.

1975 Portobello A really horrible type of training session which nobody enjoyed. In the afternoon to Oxgangs. I was up at the Blades' (6/6 Oxgangs Avenue) for an hour and a half catching up on their family news. Gail Blades and I are going to meet for coffee sometime. I watched Poldark at Mum's, had some lunch then drove back to Porty to begin reading 'Jaws' in my bed.

1976 Portobello I ran with sub 4 minute miler Adrian Weatherhead all the way in training. In the afternoon we went out to Carrington and did some driving practice. Is a sports car really the best vehicle for this? However whatever the weather it's always lovely to be out in the deep Midlothian countryside; mid-winter is as lovely as any other season; the beech hedges are still dressed in their clothes of fading bright brown leaves and many of the fields are now under the plough. Late afternoon just before dusk began to fall we travelled out to the Pentlands to enjoy afternoon tea. And then home. Under a sparkly sky.

1977 Portobello My first day back training after being side-lined with the cold for several days. At ten o'clock Joan and I went up to the Lilywhites Princes Street sale - grandmother and grandson battling it out amongst the crowds! I bought her a pair of trousers as a Christmas present and I picked up a T-shirt; thereafter next door to Murray Bros. where we both got a jumper each. With it being my first day back I took it pretty easy and ran a 150s session with Olympian Dave Wilson and Kevin McGuire. Dave's back home for his annual festive holiday to visit his parents in Edinburgh. Because my cold is still there I ran very much within myself whereas poor Dave was out the box at the end feeling sick and dizzy. It shows the difference between our different metabolisms but also the progress I've made since I first came along as a wee boy five years ago admiring Dave and his best friend David Jenkins. Dave was amusing us all with his tales of a three weeks trip to Venezuela back in October and of his adventures in the prostitute belt and on how to avoid and keep away from them. I was also speaking to Bob who is working on a 25000 word dissertation on local county councils. In the afternoon I skimmed several chapters of Charles Lipsey's Economics textbook. In the evening I enjoyed the first part of a superior programme called 'Washington behind Closed Doors'. I am fascinated by American politics. Thereafter I sat on the big old squishy armchair enjoying Grandma Joan's delicious home-made (cake-like) Christmas shortbread and continued to read Mr David Niven interspersed with pauses for laughter as I chuckled away.

1980 Portobello A longish lie in bed before collecting the Sunday newspapers from Swann's Newsagent's. I spent the morning working on my dissertation on sponsorship in sport. On my run I felt I was just plodding along feeling heavy especially with the wind against me. Come the evening lonely old me took myself off to church – Charlotte Chapel. During the service I was thinking about the whole concept of religion and feeling rather cynical about it all. I sat up late reading and watching the box before settling down to listen to an excellent radio programme 'When Soft Voices Die' by Roger Frith about the tragic story of his father in the trenches in 1917 including a poem about the ghastliness and horrors of it all.

1981 The Northlands Martha and I walked from Dochamaluaig to Strathpeffer. Neither of us felt 100%. But we enjoyed ourselves. Because of the big thaw the ground along the farm track was slippy as far as Fodderty Primary School. The snows of Saturday now no more. It took us around an hour to get to Strathpeffer and to Mackay's Hotel for a pub lunch of lentil soup and fish chips 'n peas all washed down with a cider and Babycham. Walking back we felt slightly light-headed joisting with each other in silly daft little ways.

1982 Portobello The start of the Edinburgh Sales today. I skipped about from shop to shop. The streets were mobbed. I picked up a couple of books at Old Tom's Store. In the evening Yohanan and I had a couple of games of pool at The Good Companions. Oh, Martha telephoned this morning. Fondly. She's back on Thursday evening – maybe.

1983 Powderhall I went into work this morning to the Scottish Episcopal Church coughing and spluttering enough to win a Hollywood Oscar. I was sent home at lunchtime – HURRAH! Back to the flat to pick up a few clothes before travelling out to Oxgangs. I spent a pleasant evening through at Lee's.

1984 Powderhall Logan-Smith gave me a poor reference from the Scottish Episcopal Church for my new job at Midlothian District Council. I don't mean in terms of me being a poor employee. Indeed it was rather the opposite. But it was the poor structure of it reflecting a lack of thought, judgement and imagination not focusing on some of my skills either. It read more like a report card for a primary school pupil. I gave him 3/10 for effort. A pity though. Lunchtime saw six of us go out for a bite to Clarendon Crescent. Caroline was across and looking well – very smartly dressed; was it my imagination but she seemed a little quieter and less confident than normal – not shy but perhaps demure. Jackie was in excellent form and helped to keep things chugging along nicely; she kindly bought us all some wine. Late afternoon we got away at four o'clock – it's the little things in life. I did a weights session through at Lee R.'s before spending some of the evening reading another 100 pages of Jimmy Boyle's diaries 'The Pain of Confinement' through to 2.00 am; I'm finding I have much empathy for him. Earlier I'd spent a couple of hours in at Mum's watching the last episode of the enjoyable Miss Marple. Afterwards Lee and I had a late night discussion on our philosophies of life. Martha comes back to Edinburgh tomorrow – HURRAH!

1986 Oxgangs This evening Lee; Ray; Yohanan and I went for a game of snooker. A surprisingly flat evening: Lee irritated at the hold Audrey has over Yohanan. I managed a gentle run this morning and feel somewhat stiff for it.

1988 Morningside (5.00 pm) Martha will be arriving back from The Northlands and the Highlands in the next hour or so. I'm not long back in from delivering some chairs into Mum's where I enjoyed a cup of tea and slice of cake. I telephoned Yohanan earlier – he'd been out to Vogrie Country Park: I'm playing snooker with him tomorrow. I managed to post copies of 'The Prime of Jean Brodie' by Muriel Spark and 'The Country Girls' by Edna O'Brien to Ann Dimitrov in Bulgaria. I've spent much of the last 24 hours enjoying reading my Christmas present, 'The Brothers Powys' by Richard Perceval Graves.

1990 Morningside After some very heavy rain today all the snow has gone. If there had been an overnight frost Edinburgh would have turned into an ice rink and ground to a halt. The good thing about the United Kingdom is that being an island, weather-wise nothing remains the same for too long. I saw Dr Sharon Gilmour about my throat. She prescribed Amoxil. I like her and may continue to see her. She's severe but with laced with a whiff of humour. I drove Yohanan out to Corstorphine where he bought a set of new golf irons for £99. Later I went in to town on my own – pandemonium with queuing traffic so much so I was awaiting the Ford Escort XR3i overheating. I bought Martha her present at Debbenhams – a briefcase.

1993 Colinton Martha's sister took the boys home at lunchtime without a by-your-leave. She just upped and left abruptly and didn't thank me or say goodbye. I guess that like fish after three days she goes off. On every visit here it's been the same with her – she and the boys have a lovely break from Ullapool and then she leaves in such an abrupt manner. Martha and I had a quiet lunch before going down to the Cameo to watch 'The Piano', a somewhat depressing film. A thaw on earlier. Now a tad colder. Martha is through in the kitchen making macaroni. Work beckons tomorrow.

1995 Colinton Still no indication at work on which way the wind is blowing on Local Government Re-organisation – Cath said that last Friday there was a panic with the new Director's secretary called through to type out the new structure.

The Fifth Day of Christmas
29th December

1971 Oxgangs Another lovely winter's day which allowed us all to get out for another game of football first thing. Just before dinnertime a group of us including Boo-Boo and Ali decided to go for a long cycle ride. We cycled all the way down to Portobello for a whistle stop visit to Joan's. I've never been out so far on the bike at this time of the year - just shows you. Apart from the dynamo on Dougie's bike the rest don't have any lights so we were keen to cycle back before dusk fell. Another day packed full of exercise so it was no wonder I went to Rissi's for some chips - this must be my longest gap on the chips front of 1971. On the way back down Oxgangs Street I bumped in to Mr Rigby...oh no!

1972 Portobello Thomas Graham's was an absolute breeze today. We all went out for a meal as it was the last working day of the year and just over three months since I left Boroughmuir to start working. I tasted whisky for the very first time. I didn't really like it and felt a bit tipsy for an hour or so afterwards. We got away reasonably early so I won't be back along Balcarres Street until next year. I went down to Meadowbank and did a good training session plus some weights and then my usual exercises before bed. However before going back to Porty Paul and I went in to watch the Boroughmuir Basketball team's Christmas Tournament where I saw my old Techy teacher.

1973 Portobello After my late night I slept in my bed until eleven o'clock. I walked up to Dougie's then we picked up Duncan and went to the Queen's Drive annual EAC races. In the evening I watched part one of 'Cleopatra'.

1977 Portobello Today was a rest day but some interesting developments on the home front. I drove up to the West End and went shopping. Princes Street was bustling with the crowds. I picked up some clothes; books and the Business Game. We played 'Monopoly' all afternoon. From there I went for a pint with Alistair Hutton who's travelling out to Spain tomorrow along with Chris Black, Meg Ritchie and Stewart Togher. Whilst out Roger Jenkins had phoned from London so I unfortunately missed him: *'Washington behind Closed Doors'* was excellent once again.

1978 Portobello Joan and I did some messages at Safeways. Darby wasn't too well and the doctor has sent him to the Eastern General Hospital. Despite the light snow after lunch I did a run. Whilst out the snow got heavier and as the day progressed it got colder and colder. It was like an ice age had descended. I went out in the evening for a short run partly just for the fun in being out. Winter has come.

1983 Powderhall The highlight of the day was the debut of the electric blanket that Janey had given us for our Christmas. It was a big event. To make the most of it Martha danced around naked before diving into bed bursting out laughing with excitement as she met with the warmth and heat of the bedclothes inciting me to join in the fun. She'd arrived back safely from the northlands. We'd both been looking forward to seeing each other and walked happily back from the bus station at St Andrew's Square to the flat. I'd arrived back earlier in the day to heat up the place and to bake a nutty slab. It was good to be back together. A simple cooked tea and the evening in together – all very good.

Two Days After

Will not. Cannot. Contribute anymore

One time Too many

The straw that broke the camel's back

The ounce that tipped the scales

The punch that took the fighter out

The winter's sun that fails

Night promised a sunless dawn
A lonely journey's end
Thoughtless words were last words
This man, can't make it mend
Afraid There's no storybook ending
No sorcerer's magic wand
Can resurrect this Quixote
With horse, shield and sword
This time
You drained the well
Hell!
But it's true

Someone
Some Christmas
Some day
Some words
Some say

Some girl
Some boy
Some time
Some joy

Some shallowness
Some friend
Some journey
Some end

1985 Powderhall A cold frosty morning out with St Margaret's Loch covered in ice. I was surprised at the number of people out in the park this morning. I took John for more messages at Safeways. Mum was wrapped up on the couch with the cold. Yesterday was probably her worst day. Martha arrived back at 3.00 pm. Nell and Richard looked in. Martha asked if I had a headache and then if I was making a cup of tea – 'No I'm making the lunch.' 'Oh well I think we'll just be off!' says Nell. The normal start to things. I enjoyed 'Ghandi'.

1986 Oxgangs Having a bit spare time and as a wee change I looked into West Port Books which on a winter's day with the open fire burning was a pleasant wee interlude. I was lucky too picking up a first edition of *Venture into the Interior'* by Laurens van der Post – serendipity having just enjoyed Jonathan Stedall's wonderful feature programme about him. In the morning John; Mother; Áine and I collected the keys for Morningside from the solicitors supposedly to make measurements but really to get a key made to allow us future access whilst the deal progresses through and to allow John entry. Going by the size of the key you would think I'd just bought a castle such is its size – I've never seen anything quite like it. Seeing the flat in the cold light of day rather than on that dark Friday 17th October evening with Mum when the place was half lit and looked like something out of Miss Haverham's I'm still glad I've bought it: it just needs an enormous amount of work. But perhaps not quite as much wall-papering as I'd first thought. I also have a view onto the Blackford and the Braid Hills – possibly the Pentlands too but as it's misty out I can't quite say yet (it didn't). In the late afternoon, snow began to fall; it's really only lying slightly out here at Oxgangs in the lea of the Pentland Hills.

1995 Colinton Tristan confirmed what Niall had said that the new Designate-Director had been scrapping with the Chief Executive for more money. I'm hoping that with R.S.'s departure to perhaps do well out of it despite the potential of a horrific amount of work being thrown in my direction but a few extra thousand pounds a year would make a tremendous difference with a wain on the way and the prospect of four mouths to feed. Here at West Mill the trees are enshrouded in a crust of white ice – it's straight out of a fairy-tale but I do wonder whether my garden is the coldest in all of Edinburgh. A pleasant Friday evening in with all the family along for a Chinese carry out and a game of 'Trivial Pursuits'.

The Sixth Day of Christmas

30th December

1971 Oxgangs After all the good write-ups the past few days and me saying how great the holidays have been, well today was a boring day. As I'Tve written before it's funny the way that one day everyone comes out to play and then for no apparent reason everyone just stays in. There's not really any decent daytime telly on with us being past Christmas and the evening's fayre was nothing to write about. There was a Brigitte Bardot film on but it was shite.

1972 Portobello I took part in the Edinburgh Athletic Club annual Queen's Park Drive race at Arthurs Seat but ran absolutely rubbishly. It was a bit disappointing having committed to training regularly over the past month but I ran dismally finishing towards the back of the field – in fact I may even have been last. However a much more enjoyable evening playing indoor 5 a side football with some of the older guys - Scott Brodie John Kerr, etc. I scored six goals and was pretty dominant; I'm probably doing the wrong sport with the running. Afterwards I came home to Porty for a bath.

1976 Portobello I went to see *'The Nutcracker'* ballet. It was exquisite and Tchaikovsky's score quite wonderful.

1977 Portobello Joan and I picked up some messages at Safeways then I went up to James Thin where I'm afraid I spent £12 on books however I've picked up a tremendous workbook to accompany Lipsey on Economics which I had no idea even existed. I also looked into the Lothian Region Education Department to apply to sit some Highers next May. The Lipsey is a great boon and I worked on it into the late-evening. Only Darby and I were in. I wrote a letter of athletics advice to Simon Pickles at St Andrew's University before settling down to watch an excellent 'Kojak' movie 'Summer of Sixty-Nine' followed by 'Klute'. I telephoned Dad. I'm going to spend Hogmanay (tomorrow) through at Livingstone with him. To bed at 1.00 am.

1978 Portobello In parts the snow was at least six inches deep. I managed to run a couple of miles just for the sake of doing something but it was tough going with the snowflakes stinging my eyes. I was pleasantly surprised to receive £34 from the Employment Agency in the post this morning, £20 of which I'll put straight into the bank. Despite the conditions I took the car out but it got stuck going up Lothian Road but I fortunately managed to get it moving again. We picked up some Chinese food at Mountcastle and watched Jack Lemmon in 'The Apartment' making up in the best possible way. It was so very cold we slept together in my bed. In fact it was so cold I forgot to mention that one of the windscreen wipers snapped off when I accidentally put the switch on at full speed.

1980 Portobello A strange sort of a day -the penultimate day before tomorrow and the passing of the old year. Whilst running along Portobello Promenade I ran out of energy and ended up just walking and then managed a wee jog home to Durham Road. I worked on my dissertation and then walked the dog. Outwith the wind is howling but generally it's been a good winter thus far with no snow. A swim at Porty Baths and then a little bit of the box whilst flicking through Joe Grimond's Memoirs.

Midnight: I'm delighted to hear Robin Day has received a knighthood.

1981 The Northlands My throat etc. is still quite bad so no exercise today and a long lie in bed. After lunch Martha's father dropped us off in The Northlands and we spent an hour or two wandering around the shops; for fun I also dropped into the Job Centre whilst Martha went to the bank and the post office. We had coffee at a very dilapidated coffee shop. I suspect there's an opening for a decent sized such shop in the town. We walked the couple of miles back to Northlands but not the best of country roads to be on with the swift moving occasional traffic. It could have been a dull afternoon but was actually good fun. As we walked home we talked and laughed. A relaxing evening in - 'A sad apology for a boyfriend.'

1982 Oxgangs/Portobello Some exercise then playing things by ear not leaving Oxgangs until five o'clock. Home for an hour and then up to the bus station to meet my darling girl at eight o'clock in the evening coming off the Inverness bus. We celebrated our week apart.

1984 Oxgangs I was wearing my chef's hat this evening. Mother had asked if I'd cook this evening's Sunday family meal for her and John, Áine and Spieler. A fairly average effort. Yohanan and his boys arrived shortly afterwards Along with Lee we slipped up to the

Goodies. Lee was rather depressed but came round towards evening's close whilst Yohanan remained subdued and to put the tin lid on it all I had a bit of a headache probably all brought on by this morning's rushing around – launderette, training messages, etc.

1989 Morningside I watched the Edinburgh v South rugby match at Myreside with Dad and Roddy. Dad has invited Martha and me out to Livingstone on January 2nd for a meal. In the evening Martha and I went along to a games night at Lucille's which was okay; Martha was embarrassing me about me starting to lose my hair a little – I thought it below the belt. When I raised it with afterwards she threw a wobbler.

1990 Colinton (9.30 a.m.) I've been sitting reading in bed for the past couple of hours. Fearty is sitting on the window-sill looking out at the snow. Yes it's back – we awoke to it yesterday morn. Only an inch or two but it's frozen over, with the roads quite bad. Yesterday en-route to taking Mum and John shopping at Safeways I noticed that a 16 bus had crashed on a patch of Redford Road that I hadn't been looking forward to driving over. Dad came over at lunchtime and despite the raw conditions we both thoroughly enjoyed watching a 20-20 draw between Edinburgh and Glasgow at Murrayfield. On the spur of the moment along with Mum and Yohanan the four of us went for a Chinese meal at Morningside Drive. Dad paid for it which was very generous of him. He was in excellent form taking the leading part in the table conversation and yet when I think about it Mum; Yohanan and I were equally voluble too. Mum had been somewhat fed up beforehand so the suddenness of the occasion added to her enjoyment. All that was missing was Áine for the family to have all been back together once again. Mum thought the old boy didn't look too bad buoyed up once again by the sheer force of his spirit and his joie de vivre. I was on the telephone to Martha. She is snowed in up in The Northlands but reckons that Robbie will tackle the trip southwards today. Nell also phoned later on from Muir of Ord; poor Richard has shingles. On the way back to Oxgangs my conscience antennae rang out or is it my fear? The Colinton tramp was out, slowly walking past Redford Barracks at 8.30 pm on a dreadfully cold evening. The wind was blowing in off the Pentlands – a really cutting winter's night. After putting some petrol in the car I bought him a packet of chocolate biscuits and gave him a pound. He took them both. I think that may act as an ice-breaker allowing me to speak to him in future to see if there's anything I can do for him. God knows where he shelters for the night. I once saw him many years ago on the Pentland Hills up beyond Bonaly way. As we move towards the end of the year I want to get this diary out of the way. In the following pages are cuttings which I've inserted into the journal over the past few months.

1995 Colinton As we move toward the end of the year I was reflecting on just how wonderful family life is. I decadently sat back on the sofa watching a little athletics and some rugby half-watching wee Atticus playing quite happily with his garage, cars and riding his tractor. As Martha says he's becoming such a big boy. Perhaps it's the sparseness of his hair that keeps him looking like a baby. We played along with his cousins Caomhog and Lulu together out in the back garden on his Christmas sledge. There was much hilarity and squeaks of delight and laughter and a few scrapes too. On one occasion Atticus and Lulu went careering down the garden shooting straight through the bushes and over the steps on the Snake Path all the way down to the foot of the garden. And then later a heart in the mouth moment when I lifted Atticus out of a rose bush with a small nick between his eye and nose with just the merest hint of blood. Martha said how spunky he is. We dropped the girls off in Porty after looking briefly into Yohanan's. The temperature outside is at last beginning to rise.

The Seventh Day of Christmas
Hogmanay 31st December

1971 Oxgangs It was a boring last day of 1971. The only wee excitement was going along to the chemist's shop to collect my photographs. There's always that wee bit of excitement to see how they've turned out. It's been interesting keeping a diary all year - it's one of the better things that I've done and I haven't missed a single day. I've enjoyed doing it so much that I bought a new 1972 Letts Schoolboys Diary at Baird's Newsagents and already I can't wait to put pen to paper. It's been a very mixed and varied year. On the positive side it was good that Mum got a divorce and Dad's essentially out of our lives - life at 6/2 is much much happier and it's been great having lots of our pals round. Mum always makes them feel very welcome and she's popular with the likes of Boo-Boo, Ali and Paul. Although I've not attended Meadowbank much recently I've enjoyed going along with Paul and I've made up my mind to start attending regularly and training hard with Mr Walker's sessions. It's also been great becoming such good friends with Paul Forbes. Although I've known him for years we've paired up well becoming best pals - it's almost as if where we might be a wee bit doubtful of ourselves when we're on our own but when we get together we're quite a positive combination and generally I think we're pretty good for each other. The only blot on my copybook is the schooling or should I say the lack of it. I've missed half the year through skiving and as I've recorded that's not an exaggeration. It's been a complete flipping disaster and I know I'm likely to have to leave Boroughmuir next summer without an O Level to my name and thereafter sink into oblivion. Ironically I feel sorrier for my relatives and their disappointment rather than worrying myself. If I think about it too much I just switch off and generally just park the subject. Hogmanay was transformed come the evening because we all went down to Andy 'n Maggie Ross's annual party at 6 Henderson Row. We had a ball of a time and I was drunk for the first time. After the midnight bells rang out we walked along the Dickensian streets of Stockbridge to 14 Dean Park Street where we were staying the night at Nana Pepys's. Strange isn't it we don't see her all year apart from on Christmas and Hogmanay. Happy New Year everyone - on to a new diary.

1972 Portobello I did my last training session of the year up at Meadowbank. I've really got into the running since leaving Oxgangs on St Andrew's Night doing my most sustained period of training ever. Afterwards I had a relaxed day and a bath before meeting up with Yohanan and Paul to go to the Ross's Hogmanay party at 6 Henderson Row. Both Paul and Yohanan were stoned. As Paul was waving a cheery goodbye to our hosts on their doorstep four stolen cans of beer gradually slid down and dropped out of his jacket sleeve falling downwards one by one on to the stony floor in stony silence; it was as if time had stood still - a moment frozen in time with the clock-hands still. I laughed out loud which broke the silence; as they say you have tae laugh which we boys did on the night bus back home to Oxgangs. But we had a brilliant time and lots of laughs. We walked up Dundas Street to Princes Street where we managed to get a number 2 night bus home to Oxgangs. Paul and I stayed overnight - it was fun being back at Oxgangs again. On to a new diary. 1973 awaits. I wonder what Retep's future holds?

1973 Portobello I had a real long lie in bed until eleven o'clock. I went up to Meadowbank at two. Dave Walker bought me two cups of coffee. After training I had a shower and then Scott Brodie ran Keith Ridley and me home. I left home about seven – Áine and Yohanan were already down to stay the night. Twenty of us took a pub crawl up the Royal Mile; mostly the usual suspects who meet up at the Waverley Bar at weekends. We started at Jenny Ha's and worked our way up the Royal Mile. Just after the pubs closed at ten o'clock we split up into small groups to go for a bite to eat. I was with Dougie McLean; Alistair Grant and his girlfriend Elspeth; we managed to find a table and got some Chinese food. We were late back but luckily all managed to reconvene later at the Mound and went up to the Tron Church to hear the bells and welcome in New Year 1974. I kissed Pat and Mary. Thereafter we all headed down to Coach Walker's house at 54 East Claremont Street until 2.00 am Paul and I had to sprint for the number 2 night bus which took us all the way out to Oxgangs. We bumped into Lee and Steve Westbrook before going to our beds at 3.30 a.m.

1974 Portobello A few phone calls this morning and an afternoon training session. Stevie Greene's up. Dave Cocksedge is sending me forms for an American college. I took a couple of jackets out to Oxgangs for Yohanan. Thereafter I was bored so I gave Aileen Gordon a ring. We met at Helen Golden's flat, had a drink then went back to her house. We sat up until 4.00 am on New Year's morning playing records. Her mum tried without success to get me a taxi however taking pot luck when I left her home I got one immediately at the top of the road. Well Retep that's another year and to be honest it's been pretty fantastic. Everything's happened. Here's hoping that 1975 is going to be even better.

Sea Fever

I must go down to the seas again to the lonely sea and the sky

And all I ask is a tall ship and a star to steer her by;

And the wheel's kick and the wind's song and the white sail's shaking

And a grey mist on the sea's face and a grey dawn breaking.

I must go down to the seas again for the call of the running tide

Is a wild call and a clear call that may not be denied;

And all I ask is a windy day with the white clouds flying

And the flung spray and the blown spume and the sea-gulls crying.
I must go down to the seas again to the vagrant gypsy life
To the gull's way and the whale's way where the wind's like a whetted knife;
And all I ask is a merry yarn from a laughing fellow-rover
And quiet sleep and a sweet dream when the log trick's over.

John Masefield

1976 Portobello I was keen to repeat previous Christmas Eves experiences and went down to Gullane Sands in the Triumph Spitfire on this the last day of the year. In the evening Yohanan and I went for some drinks to The Steading Inn at Hillend; then to The Buckstone; and on to the Hunters Tryst before going down to the Walkers' Hogmanay party. We got home at 2.00 am. We had a wonderful time. The years seem to be getting better and better; happy days.

1977 Portobello Late morning there was a surprisingly large group of us out for our 300 metres session - Norrie; John Scott; Paul; Adrian and me. However with the after-effects of the cold I had to drop out after only six runs; possibly the first time I've dropped out of a session; it doesn't augur well given I'll be racing both Paul and John over the half mile at the AAA's Championships in January. I dropped Paul off up at the Bridges and drove home through a quiet Arthurs Seat reflecting on the year gone by and the year ahead with the uncertain promise of the 1978 Commonwealth Games in Edmonton and the European Championships behind the Iron Curtain in Prague. Given Steve Ovett has a personal best of 1 minute 45.4 seconds and Sebastian Coe is the current number one Brit am I getting just a little ahead of myself given my best is a pedestrian 1 minute 53 seconds from an indoors Perth run three years ago? I'm crossing the Rubicon so 'Let the dice fly high!' Having driven back in a reflective dwam (to paraphrase Robert Louie from Catriona) I arrived back home. We sat and played 'Monopoly' and then had a lot of fun making up an imaginary guest list for our wedding - who's in and who's out. I phoned Dad and in between Paul phoned several times; later we collected Paul and Lorraine and went to the local Three Inns; as I was driving I only had one small drink but we had a lot of fun and laughter at

TheGreat Wall Restaurant in Portobello. The waitresses didn't quite know what to make of Paul who was gently outrageous. Very late on I went to a party at Dad's.

1978 Portobello The conditions are of course terrible out with thick snow lying all around and the worse weather for years. And here we are, the last day of the year. Earlier on we'd got some food from Portobello and bumped into Davie Reid on his way to The Sands Hotel. Back at the house there was some bad news awaiting us that put me off eating anything. The hospital had just phoned to say that Darby was not responding to treatment. It came as quite a shock. We sat up late to see in the New Year but not with much heart. I had a bad feeling what might happen. And sure enough at three o'clock the phone rang out piercing the night air. I knew what it was before Aunt Dottle even looked in to tell me. Darby had passed away in his sleep. What more can I say?

1980 Portobello Well it was a very flat end to the year and to the decade too. Rather than going out in a sparkle it fizzled out. In the evening I had a bad headache and felt sick so I was unable to attend the (Ronnie) Brownes' New Year party at Wester Coates Gardens. I was disappointed as I was looking forward to going along and mingling with everyone. As for the last day of the year it was quite wild with the wind howling, heavy showers of rain and the occasional burst of snow-flakes. I trained once; did some work on my dissertation and spent a large part of the day playing the 'Business Game' on the basis that it relates to my course as well as being fun too; the best strategy would appear to be to build up just enough cash to thereafter commence a shipping company.

1981 The Northlands The year I met Martha. It's the end of 1981 and my eleventh diary in a row. The death of the old year is sad but it was getting tired. I'm excited about the New Year and the good things that it may bring. How should I sum up the year? Well: Satisfying in eventually obtaining a qualification (Bachelor of Arts degree) although some people may say 'about time too!'; but it's been a long journey since leaving Boroughmuir School with 2 O Levels back in 1972; Demoralising at not finding employment and establishing a career and making some money; Thankful in finding a new love, more beautiful than I once knew; Melodramatic and fragile at the thought of losing Martha; Memorable for some of the days and the outings and the events; Enjoyable for reading some excellent books including Buchan; Bader; Fischer, et al; Paul getting married; Joan having her own art exhibition; Martha and me passing our exams. And as for the last day of the year it was a bit up and down. In the afternoon I walked through the fields on my own; in the evening Martha treated me to a lovely meal at the Craigdarroch Lodge Hotel Contin. Have we arranged to meet there a year hence? At 3.00 am on New Year's morning Martha dragged me out of bed to go up to Strathpeffer to pick up Bruce – luckily I'm the good-humoured type.

1982 Portobello The last day of the year. Another year. Gone by, just like that. Martha and I felt rather happy and excited – just one of those days when everything just whizzed by. Town. And buscards and Joan's messages. Late afternoon I organised a meal and an evening out. Yohanan was delighted to see me. Spieler picked Martha and me up at 7.30 pm to travel out to Oxgangs. I felt sorry for Aunt Dottie – without a partner it's particularly hard for her at this time of the year. Mum was asleep. Six of us – Yohanan and K.; Áine and Spieler; and Martha and me went down to the New Peking Chinese Restaurant for a lovely meal although I found I was having to work hard to keep the conversation flowing. But overall I think everyone enjoyed themselves; thereafter we headed out to the Steading Inn at Hillend in the lea of the Pentland Hills. Oxgangs for some coffee then down to Jack Nixon's Hogmanay party at Brighton Crescent at Portobello. I've just first-footed Joan and Aunt Dottie; Jimmy Paul from across the road looked in later. Bed at 2.00 a.m.

1983 Oxgangs Well that's us heading into 1984 so I thought I better write at least write something to finish off 1983. I haven't been quite so assiduous at keeping my diary this year. The weather out was terrible with torrential rain which just poured down. I went out on the Lothian Road – shades of RLS from a century ago – with Lee and co. Originally we'd intended to go up to the Tron (Church) but by 10.30 pm the pubs had closed and we just grabbed some pie and chips and headed homeward to bring in the New Year at his parents' home at Oxgangs Avenue. I looked into Mum's. Unfortunately I had a migraine-type headache, was sick and ended up just going to bed – shades of a couple of years back when I had to miss Ronnie Browne's party I'd thought of telephoning Martha (in the Highlands) but didn't. She too thought/hoped I might have; I wish now I had.

1984 Powderhall Poor Martha was back to the workhouse this morning (Monday). In a token gesture I staggered out of bed at 7.20 am to make her breakfast but she sent me back to bed. That's about all I recall and I didn't get up until a couple of hours later for a short run, bath and breakfast. Martha called me around 11.30 am. I went up to town but I wasn't really interested so I jumped on a bus down to Portobello. Joan was busy about the house doing a bit of cleaning to see the New Year in. Over a bowl of soup we enjoyed a wee chat. She was telling me that Margaret had dropped by yesterday to see her. I did a little bit of exercise in at Meadowbank and saw Bill Walker for a minute or two. He's having a few people round this evening. I prepared some chili con carne for Martha's dinner whilst she phoned Joan to thank her for the homemade sweets and the present of the home-made doll. Later she was on the blower to Nell. Lucille and Dave popped round (from Rodney Street) for a drink with us.

1986 Oxgangs Because of my cold etc. I really didn't feel like going out. I played snooker with Lee for a few hours. Back at Oxgangs it was nice to see Dad who'd been round for a couple of hours. I've told him I'll visit him in the New Year. Amelia had phoned several times so I went to a party at her friend Karen's flat at 12.30 am and stayed there for several hours.

1988 Morningside My cold rages on - blocked up, running nose, etc. with each day worse than the preceding one. I seem to have had something wrong on each day throughout the month of December. Last evening we had Dad; Bett; Roddy; Yohanan and Audrey up for a game of 'Trivial Pursuits'. They enjoyed themselves, Yohanan in particular, who partnered Martha to a win. Dad enjoyed himself too and as ever was in good form. I was surprised at how much Chinese he managed to pack away.

1989 Morningside Auld Year's Night This morning I read that the Scotland rugby cap, Peter Steven has retired from district rugby; funny to read that as yesterday when I was watching him play I thought that he must be getting on a bit and also that he's slowing up.

1990 Colinton Well, Christmas came and went. Mum, John, Aunt Dottle and Joan stayed through until Saturday and thoroughly enjoyed themselves. Simple pleasures such as a warm shower were a real treat for Joan. Yohanan stayed intermittently - long enough to consume large quantities of vodka, rum and whisky. Martha arrived back from the Highlands later in the day – both of us glad to get back into a routine. This evening along with Nell and Richard we're going round to Lucille's for a meal and a games night. Something to do.

Later A pleasant Hogmanay at Lucille's with six or seven other couples along and an enjoyable game of 'Outburst'. Home at 2.30 am, the Edinburgh streets busy.

1993 Colinton I've never been one for summing up the year gone by so I'm hardly likely to start now. But I should record that we got married this year and Martha and I have never been happier together. I loved hearing her say a few weeks ago that as she walked along Princes Street one Saturday she thought how happy she was – the happiest she had ever been. It brought me great joy and made my heart sing out. For her it was the combination of being married and expecting our first child together. I spent much of today at the office clearing out an amazing number of files. And then come the evening the same exercise through in the library. Martha set forth at five o'clock to collect Nell and Richard whilst I remained in Edinburgh. I was worried about her driving such a long way northward on icy roads so I was glad and relieved when she phoned around nine o'clock. Mum phoned. And then Yohanan later on from Áine's for quite a while with the lovely sound of Áine's girls hovering in the background and laughing away – I couldn't quite get over how Caomhog sounded on the phone. I sat up until 2.00 am just pottering around.

1995 Colinton The last day of another year. It seems quite amazing that come tomorrow wee Atticus enters his third calendar year. This past year has been the happiest of our lives. Atticus has brought us the most enormous amount of pleasure. Martha was saying what a delightful age he is at just now – 20 months. He really is a character and inter-relates with us so well. He is incredibly huggable and it's such a pleasure to be able to have a laugh with him and give him a big squeeze. Whilst he is somewhat monosyllabic his vocabulary is now quite extensive. Being a father is a remarkable experience and it's something I wouldn't have missed for the world. I hate to raise the wrath of the gods by my hubris but I feel it's important to record just how I feel and that if some day Atticus happens to read this journal he realises just how much Martha and I love him and what incredible joy he has brought to our world. At the swimming pool this morning there was a small development with Atticus making the slightest semblance of a doggie paddle. Martha and I are probably closer than we have ever been. Atticus has spurred us on to be better people and we have broadly similar ideas on how to bring up children and the importance of providing a secure family home filled with love. On the work front my team has been the best and most satisfying to work with. But that's all to change with hopes of further promotion.

The Eighth Day of Christmas
1st January - New Year's Day

1978 Portobello After a lovely buffet at Mum's we drove back in the dark and cold to Portobello; however disaster was about to strike. Just as we approached the traffic lights at the start of Peffermill Road, Darby's car had a puncture - the rear inside wheel. The tyre deflated and didn't respond to any attempts at resuscitation. The icy wind cut straight through me further hampering any efforts on my part. Meanwhile it made sense for Grandma Joan, Aunt Dottle and Jill the dog to leap on to a passing number 42 bus much to the dog's relief! We weren't able to repair the wheel so Darby and I managed to commandeer a passing taxi and travelled home in style but not before my poor friend almost went her length on the ice with me ungentlemanly laughing at the scenario.

1979 Portobello The New Year began with the greatest sadness of all with the death of my beloved grandfather Darby. After the telephone rang Aunt Dottle came through to my room at 3.00 am to tell me the news. Although we'd been fore-warned very late-on about his condition it still came as a great shock. I found it impossible to get back to sleep. He was a wonderful grandfather to we three kids Áine, Yohanan and me. I've loved him more than anyone and have dreaded this day since I was around twelve years old. With Mum having no telephone it was a nightmare arriving on her doorstep for her annual New Year party with such news, the spectre at the feast; but despite her great distress she coped very well indeed. After lunch I took Jill (the Fox Terrier dog) out for a walk in the snow down past the Oxgangs Crescent shops and on through a very snowy Braidburn Valley. It was quite lovely out with lots of people celebrating the New Year with a healthy walk and seeing fathers playing on sledges with their children.

Postscript When we first received that late night phone call from the hospital just before the bells I should have walked through the snows to the Eastern General Hospital to be by my grandfather's bedside. Forty years on, that I didn't, still haunts me still and will to the day that I too die. I feel guilty that I didn't go to be there with him - to hold and to stroke his hand and to kiss his brow in the hours of his greatest need – not to have done so still weighs heavily. Especially when he had been like a father to me since the day I was born. But to quote Minnie Driver I was young and overwhelmed.

1984 Oxgangs Aunt Margaret (Mum's cousin) picked me up at seven o'clock in the evening and ran me out in her Lancia sports car to her Georgian country home, Stobsmills House Gorebridge. The house is so atmospheric – straight out of Dickens with oil lamps dimly lighting the hall. After a sherry by the sitting room log fire we went through to dinner. I felt like a character in a play.

1990 Morningside Outside it's damp. I opened the New Year and decade watching the Portobello Prom Race. It was pleasant to catch up with a lot of people who I haven't seen for a while - Sandy & Liz Sutherland; Alistair and Duncan Baker; Robin Morris; Adrian Weatherhead; Alan Robson; Brian Kirkwood; Bill Gentleman etc. I was really impressed with Adrian finishing second, at what 46? Thereafter I took Joan and Aunt Dottie out to Mum's at Oxgangs for the annual buffet. I enjoyed playing with Caomhog and then later the family divided in to two teams to play 'Trivial Pursuits'. Back to work on Thursday. What a thought. As for resolutions? Sometimes I like the idea of getting married. And at other times I hate it. And then there's the usual - fitness; finance; cultural; maintain weight; my journals; and to devote half an hour each day to progressing my idea for a book, 'Mainly Samuel. And Paul'.

1996 Colinton I'm sitting watching on the television the Edinburgh celebrations which are ringing in the New Year. It's great seeing our capital at the forefront with the Mons Meg cannon firing out; the fireworks pipe bands and a selection of music groups too. They estimate there are 250000 people in Princes Street. The crowds of people are hugging one another thankful for seeing in another year and determined to squeeze every bit out of life. And what of family Pepys? We're hoping for a healthy baby in the spring and a smooth birth. And to consolidate and build on what we have. At a practical level I could do with earning a little more money to help feed the extra mouth at the table. I want to mature further as a person especially around the concept of unconditional love. Our twenty month old boy Atticus has brought that very much to the fore – lighting the touch paper but it's something I want to try to extend further with family and friends. In the years ahead our wee family is going to bring us bundles of joy – it will be a privilege to spend time with them and to give, give, give. The moments when they are young will be fleeting and I am determined to savour and absorb and to enjoy it all. I also wish to continue to grow intellectually too aiming to read a book each week and then come the spring to continue creating our garden paradise. This morning there was not too much chance of a lie in. Atticus brought me my slippers shouting 'Up...up...up!' The snow and ice have disappeared apart from on the Pentland Hills and our north facing back garden that slopes down to the Water of Leith. Outside it's a little overcast with a smir of rain but still it's good to start another year afresh. For once I wasn't proactive. My step-father rang up from Oxgangs to wish us all a Happy New Year as did Grandma Joan who was most surprised that I had not rung her (669 4260) at 45 Durham Road. As my good friend Paul Forbes says, communication is a two way thing. And now more news on the baby front – Martha's best friend is pregnant too – wonderful news after we all thought she might not be able to conceive; her due date is August. I'd wandered into the sitting room to find her on the phone and in tears. I thought 'Oh fuck! her Ross-shire farmer father is dead!' but no, instead they were tears of joy. Nell is only seven weeks so it's very early indeed and we can but keep our fingers crossed that everything works out fine. But it raises lots of questions too – her partner's schedules; her own work at Lauriston not to mention how to break the news informing her estranged husband, Richard. But there's no question she will make for a very good mother indeed. T'other baby news is that our sister in law's sister had the first New Year baby in Inverness. Spur of the moment Atticus and I dropped into Mum's with some cards and golf balls for John's (her husband and my step-father) birthday on Wednesday. My sister and the girls were there having stayed overnight. She's very down; I would hazard a guess that that her husband is at the root of it all – perhaps she wants him back. Meanwhile wee Atticus certainly cheers everyone up – according to Mum 'He's a handful – shortly he'll be like his father (me) dreeping out of windows!' My brother Yohanan telephoned from work (Ferranti's). He was up to high-doe about getting his flat ready for the new carpets being fitted on Saturday. Two of my favourites from Atticus just now – the inflexion in his voice when he says 'O-kay' and when he leaves me to go upstairs to bed he says – 'Bye Dad.'

The Ninth Day of Christmas

2nd January

1978 Portobello The phone rang at 9.30 am Guess who? Wrong. It was Andy Ross (Mother's cousin) about Darby's abandoned car at Peffermill Road. Andy arrived at the house at 10.00 am and we went out to mend the puncture. He was underneath the car laying on the cold wet road putting the jack underneath and holding it in place whilst I loosened the wheel. I don't know how he managed it as it was so bitterly cold; I couldn't feel my hands. However we got the job done fairly quickly but not without a fair share of tension that the jack would remain in place and hold the car upright. Thereafter Andy came back to Durham Road for some coffee and shortie and was full of his usual good cheer making us all laugh and delighting the household. We met the gang there including our athletics coach Bill Walker; Paul Forbes; Lorraine Morris; Davie Reid, etc. It was an enjoyable day and I thought the winner Roy Heron was very impressive - 10.79 seconds for the 110 metres off 8.5 metres. After giving Paul and Lorraine a lift home I went out and ran five miles as I start to try to regain full fitness after this debilitating cold. It was good to be out and running over the wintry Duddingston Golf Course; there were only one or two golfers out so I essentially had the parkland to myself. After being in company for much of the day I enjoyed the solitariness and contemplation. As I ran through the Figgate Park on the way back I bumped into Maria - she was out walking the dog. I felt pretty knackered but I had at least run at a pretty steady pace throughout. Thereafter back home for a bath; a bowl of soup before enjoying another instalment of 'Washington behind Closed Doors'. A life in a day.

1983 Portobello I was surprised to see there were Sunday papers on sale in Edinburgh today and also that Dave Valentine had won the 800 metres at the Powderhall New Year Sprint meeting at Meadowbank – his fourth title over different distances. Later on I ran in Portobello Park after playing 15 minutes of football with a couple of youngsters. The 'Major' (because he's tall, erect and has a moustache and a military looking old raincoat) wished me a Good New Year. I was sorry to hear that old Mr Marsden had died aged 87. He just slipped away in his chair after falling asleep. He had a lot of character as he shuffled along in his beautiful fine clothes – tweed jacket and cap. I recall one summer evening when I saw him at Portobello Library with his wife. I looked at the two of them and thought how nice that they still had each other after all these years; I think it was back in the summer of '81. But as I looked at them I wondered just how long this frail and loving couple had left together. Well it wasn't so very long.

1985 Powderhall I walked Martha up to her work at Queen Street en-route passing Patterson's Electrical shop where a chap was outside sitting on a deckchair well wrapped up awaiting the start of the sales. A policeman was having a friendly chat with him. Taking a quick peak in the shop window I noticed a video recorder reduced from £400 to £15! I met Yohanan and Lee at 9.55 a.m. at the Braid Hills Golf Course. A late middle-aged man asked if he could join us. From the outset Lee was swearing away and lacing his conversation with plenty of sexual innuendo – as well really as otherwise it would have been terribly stiff and formal all the way around.

1987 Morningside I had dinner at Amelia Lanier's at her brother's flat in the Dean Village followed by a game of 'Trivial Pursuits' with several of her pals. She made a really impressive curry for us all. A pleasant evening. There is much to write – maybe later? However what about resolutions too?

The Tenth Day of Christmas
3rd January

1971 Oxgangs I got up at about 9.30 am and enjoyed a wee treat - bacon on toast for breakfast. I walked down to Colinton Mains to buy the Sunday Post. It was lovely hearing the St John's Church bell ringing out calling the community to worship. Later on we went down to Portobello to visit Joan and Darby; after dinner we went for a wee run in the Ford Zephyr down to Gullane Beach. We lost Joan (hunting for agates along the shore) but picked her up further along the road. In the evening Mum's friend John (my future step-father) came by and gave me 10 shillings towards buying my first suit. I'm now a young man. *Dr Finlay's Casebook* was on the box: Janet wails 'Oh Dr Cameron, Dr Cameron I think I've got heartburn'; Cameron thunders back 'Janet. - Get yer tit oot o' ma porage.' Well she might have!

1972 Oxgangs I didn't get up until 12.30 pm - not out of my bed until the afternoon - that must be a first. Clearly the result of my New Year's adventures catching up on me. Although we hadn't really organised it seven of us went in to town including Boo-Boo Hanlon; Paul Forbes; and my brother Yohanan. I can't recall that big a group of us going out together. We all headed into Princes Street which was surprisingly busy but I guess it's also to do with the sales and people still being on holiday and looking for something to do. We visited quite a few of the shops including Woolies at the east end. Late afternoon we came back to Oxgangs on the number 16 bus and enjoyed some cans of lager - what are we like? We also met a group of girls and I ended up kissing one of them.

1979 Portobello I picked Mum and John up at ten o'clock despite the atrocious road conditions caused by all the snow. At Greenbank I didn't think I'd make it up the hill but somehow managed to gently coax the Ford Cortina up the gradual, but steep incline. John and I registered Darby's death at Abbeyhill then had coffee at Joan's and from there we went on to the undertaker's. There was a light moment at the Registrar's when the couple in front of us were asked what her dad's occupation was – she exclaimed, 'Oh, he drove a steamroller!' Darby's funeral is on Saturday; it will be a very small affair. Later Mum, John and I saw about a wreath at Rankin's the Florist – Mum says it's a lovely wreath.

1983 London Dad drove me down to London to help me find a job. We left Livingston at eleven o'clock at night. The snow had just started to fall. It was terribly severe in parts and it must have made it very hard for Dad to drive. Meanwhile I tried to get as much sleep as possible and lay back on the reclining seat but it was impossible to sleep. I kept thinking 'What am I doing here?' It's madness. I should be by Martha's side right now snuggling up tight in bed. There was one amusing but slightly poignant moment. We had stopped for a flask of tea. Dad takes sugar in his tea and had deposited the small pouch in his hat. When he was clearing up and thought he had finished everything he replaced the hat back on his head and of course the sugar came tumbling down his face and neck. JESUS CHRIST! he exclaimed as he started going through his few strands of hair trying to extract the granules. I suppressed my desire to laugh.

The Eleventh Day of Christmas

4th January

1971 Oxgangs I enjoyed a longer lie in this morning as Yohanan was doing my milk round once again; he's a glutton for punishment. He's aged 12 years old and out 'n about pushing the milk barrow along the streets of early morning Bruntsfield. I think it's still a novelty to him but before he knows it he'll have left Firrhill School and it'll become the norm. I took my wee sister Áine into town to help get her the new specs she needs however the shop was closed. The temperature is really cold; we were going to do some cross country running but ended up having a game of football across at Oxgangs House instead; Mrs Cook said I gashed her son's leg. I don't recall it happening but feel a wee bit bad about it now. It still feels like a holiday but with the likes of 'Blue Peter' back on we're slowly reverting back to normal. Mum is actually back to work at the Civil Service Agriculture and Fisheries at Chesser House and Boroughmuir School awaits me on Wednesday. Yuck! Or should that be Yikes?

1972 Oxgangs I started my new milk round this morning at Berry's Dairy at Montpelier Place. Also it means I'm off the Dummy milk floats too and back on to a heavy metal barrow. It went pretty well partly because of the novelty of it being a new job but also because my brother Yohanan was along to help me out and of course no school today either. However, fun as it was with my considerable experience of being a working laddie I know there will be miserable cold mornings ahead. After breakfast the pair of us went into town with Paul Forbes - good fun; the three of us chum up pretty well. I spent some of my Christmas money from Dad on a new pair of baseball boots from Woolworths at Princes Street. I don't normally get them until the summer but they'll be good for doing the milk round. Talk about it being my lucky day amazingly I found a tenner - I thought all my Christmases had come at once. I treated the three of us to a wee slap up feed at Woolies Café - braw. We then went to a pawnbroker's shop in the Grassmarket where we pawned a watch for money. It was the first time Yohanan and I had ever been to one but Paul seemed to know all about them. It just shows you what you can learn from others; it was an interesting experience and the shop was full of stuff, packed to the gunnels but they don't give you the true value. Back home at Oxgangs, Ali Douglas came round to join us - he's staying the night. We watched a good pirate film called 'Raiders of the Seven Seas' featuring old Barbarossa. Our sister Áine's still not in yet.

1973 Portobello I was dead tired this morning. Ian Richards was back to work at Thomas Graham & Son Ltd. Builders & Plumbers Merchants 51 Balcarres Street; along with Scott Wallace and me we were the only members of the costing department in to work today. Being a Thursday I'd intended to work late to get some overtime monies but I changed my mind. We phoned our boss Bimbo Wallace at home and he says he's going to return to work tomorrow. I went along to the Royal Bank of Scotland at the foot of Comiston Road and took out £3. After work Scott's dad gave me a lift to Mayfield but I had to wait quite a while at the King's Buildings for the 42 bus. After tea I went up to Meadowbank and was running not badly at all. I came home with Dougie McLean however everyone was out and I had to hang about outside 45 Durham Road in the cold for half an hour until Darby Joan and Aunt Dottle came home. It meant I missed 'Colditz'. Oh and my sister Áine had been down earlier.

1975 RAF Cosford I was invited to run in the 600 metres which was televised; it was my first appearance on the box much to the delight of my grandfather who I phoned later from a transport cafe. David Coleman gave me a good crit saying how promising he thought I was. Because I was an extra I had to start behind the top American Mark Winzenreid and be in the same lane; despite being bundled off the track after 400 metres I came through well to run a U.K Junior Record.

1977 Portobello I watched our own Robert Louis Stevenson's *'Weir of Hermiston'* on the box - excellent. Overnight the temperature had been well below zero. During the morning I broke the ice on the pond; one goldfish had died so we're down to only eight now. As the hose was frozen I was back and forward re-filling the pond with buckets of water. Come two o'clock in the afternoon I ran the 2 miles to Meadowbank and did a gym circuit before venturing across to Arthurs Seat with the weights jacket on to run a good hill session. It was lovely up there. Dusk was fast approaching and the landscape glistened with a white frost that had not lifted all day. At such moments I feel at one with the world, although it was a solitary and lonely feeling too; I felt like the last man alive as there was no one else to be seen in a quiet Queen's Park.

Stopping by Woods on a Snowy Evening

'... The woods are lovely dark and deep

But I have promises to keep

And miles to go before I sleep

And miles to go before I sleep.'

Robert Frost

Afterwards I ran home, studied and saw the doctor about why I was picking up so many colds. I was impressed with him; he wonders whether it may be to do with my dry skin - an interesting theory.

1979 Portobello After yesterday there is not too much to be done; really it's just a case of waiting until Saturday for Darby's funeral.

1980 Portobello This morning I received a letter from Dad which was good because I was beginning to get a little concerned about the silence of the previous weeks. Anyway the letter was dated the 15th December so there was obviously a postal problem; the letter was posted in Annapolis in the USA. He seemed to be getting on fine and had been out meeting friends that day in the port. He sent £10 each for Áine, Yohanan and me; he's behind the times with regard to inflation.

1982 London To give Dad his due he made a sterling job of the rest of the driving to London however it was a frustrating morning in the office as Mr Dedezade didn't make an appearance – none of his staff knew where he was. We're staying at Balham at Dad's friends Ken and Joan who I stayed with back in 1979. Dad took us all out for a Chinese meal. It was very good and at what I thought were 1973 prices at least compared to Edinburgh.

Monday the 4th January

Suddenly! I can no longer appear by your side

That hurts. My impetuous nature longs to surprise you

At a Queen Street corner when your day's work is done.
Without such there's no freshness. No excitement
No well being
And no peace
I long to hold you Tight In my arms
To see that impish smile
And to watch your eyes when they say
My love I feel I feel for you my love
Come see my heart

1983 Powderhall Lee was his usual good company; every now and again he was voicing forth on life; the menu today included his former girlfriend and the love of his life Doreen who emigrated to Canada when he blew their relationship – and of how 1983 was going to be his year; and that he was feeling the cheeriest he'd been for a very long time. And on girls too. And how he'll find one soon. He's been celibate for 3 months – is this a record? All good fun though and I admire his honesty.

1988 Morningside I've had my annual Christmas/New Year heavy cold. I went out for a two hour trek from Morningside up and around Arthurs Seat. I was surprised at just how many people were on the summit – New Year Resolutions, etc.

The Twelth Day of Christmas

5th January

1971 Oxgangs My brother Yohanan did the milk run for me again this morning; it keeps me out of the boss's hair once again so I didn't get up until 10.00 am. I went down to The Store (St Cuthbert's Cooperative) at Oxgangs Road North and did the messages. I helped the old lady who lives in the next Stair (8/4 Oxgangs Avenue) by carrying her bags home for her. She's a great auld lass; she's the lady who asked Mum how Yohanan was getting on bear-hunting in Canada! - what a laddie. I played football across in the playground before Joan and Darby came out to visit us. One of Mum's best pals Mrs Marion Dibley (4/4 Oxgangs Avenue) caught me smoking; I think she'll keep stum. 'Quizball' was on telly - Ian Ure is a bright lad - well he's Scottish after all; later

'Doomwatch' was on - cool.

1980 Portobello Yohanan was already at Mum's keen to get his cheque. We went up to the bookies at Oxgangs Broadway. I placed £1 on 'Hot Tomato' which was duly squelched. We met Boo-Boo Hanlon there and went for a drink at the Goodies (The Good Companions). It was great to see Boo-Boo again. It's been awhile; he's getting married in June. He was saying he hasn't any REAL friends – people that he can just drop by and go into their homes – funny how that's become quite common these days. I looked into Meggetland and picked up a form to join Boroughmuir Rugby Club for the social scene and perhaps renew old school acquaintances; at the bus stop I bumped into Wendy Boxer. She was as effervescent as ever; it seems like only yesterday (actually 5 years) since I took her and A. out to start as freshers at university.

1982 London Ken White awoke me this morning with a mug of tea. Seeing him standing there was like going back in time to when I stayed with him and Joan when I was doing my student placement three years ago at the Seahorse Ship Management Company in the City of London. Dad finally contacted Mr Dedezade and we're to meet him this afternoon. It rained all day. I met Mr D. for several hours. We got on fairly well and there is the possibility of a job for me but it would have to be at a practical salary. He's very much a do-er – an incredible entrepreneur who will always be able to make money. He has a lot of positive characteristics. He expressed his values that if you work hard for him he will treat you fairly. I think much is also dependent on him taking a shine to you. He was patronising but went on to also admit to that trait. Anyway he wants me to think over his offer and whether I really wish to relocate to London. There was no train back to Edinburgh until the mail train at 10.30 pm. Dad treated me to a very high class Chinese meal – exquisitely rich food that I hadn't experienced before. It was a shabby third class carriage that took me back to Scotland's capital – a long and intermittent journey meant I didn't arrive back in Edinburgh until 6.00 am. I'm looking forward to seeing Martha. I can't get over just how much I've missed her.

1983 Portobello Because I'd got to bed at 4.00 am I cancelled my normal early morning run with Steven to Joppa and along the seafront to Portobello Promenade however I ended up still going out myself at 7.00 am but up to Duddingston Village which in some ways I prefer; it's the same length of time spent running but it's easier mentally. At Oxgangs, Mum was doing her dinger over husband John, who's fallen 3 months behind on making payments as well as owing cash to money lenders. I ended up being on the end of her wrath too. I continued reading Allan Massie's 'The Last Peacock'. I'm enjoying it – it drifts along very nicely.

1985 Powderhall I sat up until past midnight reading John Buchan's *'The Watcher by the Threshold'*; being fantasy it was different from some of his usual fayre but very enjoyable with many of the usual wonderful descriptions which flow so effortlessly from his pen – what craftsmanship in his descriptions of country houses, old libraries and the moors. Earlier I'd wandered down the Royal Mile looking into a couple of second-hand bookshops; I also went in to the Eastern Crafts shop and was talking to the old man who was sitting smoking his pipe. He told me that his son ventures out to Nepal, Afghanistan, etc. in search of wares to import for their business – such an interesting life. After her work Martha and I met at Low's at Logie Green Road to do some messages. Afterwards I went out for a run; as I was passing a chap aged around 35 at Warriston Graveyard I exhaled deeply and the poor chap just about leapt out of his skin! I chuckled to myself once I'd run a bit further along the path.

1986 Powderhall Once out to Oxgangs I chatted with Lee about what to do. Was it not more practical just to remain at the flat until I found a room elsewhere? He said you can be too educated and civilised about things and said I should be taking a stance - to clear out. I took his advice and collected some of my things. Martha and I managed to joke about things and she shed a tear. Once back to Oxgangs I of course immediately thought have I made a mistake - the reality sinks in - maybe I was a little hasty. Who was the Portuguese sailor (Magellan) who burnt his boats? On a lighter note Lee and I were out throwing snowballs at windows – Charlie Hanlon leant out of his top floor window (6/7 Oxgangs Avenue) thinking it was a bunch of kids shouted down that he would 'kick our arses.'

1993 Colinton I went to see the RSA Diploma Exhibition; it was fair to middling. I was taken with Charles Oppenheimer's 'Kirkcudbright under Snow'. I had lunch at Joan's. She was a little better – brighter and perkier – I had to give her a hand to remove the electrodes from the 24 hour ECG from her chest!!!

1994 Colinton I looked into Real Foods at Broughton Street to buy in some walnuts, brans, etc. It was wet all day. I enjoyed watching 'Hoffa' on the box – that period of American history has long fascinated me. It seemed to me that Danny DeVito got the balance right – of a flawed individual who had been well motivated with an appreciation of organisational reality.

Twelfth Night
6th January

1971 Oxgangs Crazy; I got up at 4.00 am to do my milk run getting back home to Oxgangs on the number 16 bus at 6.30 am. I then went back to bed and did not wake up again until 11.00 am. Crikey that's me missed the first day of the new Boroughmuir school-term - an inauspicious (good word) start - and BANG goes one of my New Year Resolutions. Instead I did housework tidying up giving the place a good scrub. Later on I played football; watched 'Star Trek' - excellent as ever featuring the last man on a planet a mysterious old librarian - all followed by a relaxing bath. I need to be looking good for school tomorrow.

1972 Oxgangs I finished my milk round at 8.00 am so it was a pretty quick turnaround as I was back to Boroughmuir today. If you forget the exams that's really the first time I've been back through the Boroughmuir school gates since November and yet no-one said anything. Is it any wonder that I continue to suit myself as to whether I bother turning up or not? And just to make things worse it was a boring day at school and I haven't done very well in my exams whereas my peers are disappointed if they only get a mark above 80% - just how do they do that? After school Yohanan, Paul Forbes and I played table tennis then took the number 16 bus down to the Leith Sparta Boxing Club where Paul used to train; however it was closed - a bit of a wasted journey but we had a good laugh on the buses. Back home to 6/2. Some bad news - Ali Douglas (8/3 Oxgangs Avenue) has lost his dog; we gave him a hand to look for it but no joy. There's a hell of a racket going on out the back. I don't ever recall mentioning that in my diary.

1978 Portobello I went up to Meadowbank Sports Centre to have a chat with my athletics coach Bill Walker to discuss my training and competition plans. He mentioned a possible trip to Estepona

Spain in April with the UK national coach John Bailey. After lunch I studied before going for a run around Duddingston Golf Course; as I ran through the Figgate Park I saw a young girl from Edinburgh Southern Harriers out for a walk. I still feel tired from last evening. I studied until 7.30 p.m. We got the Christmas photos back – they're super – Mum wants six of them. We then went out to The Steading at Hillend at the foot of the Pentland Hills for a drink and then on to the Mei-Kwei Chinese Restaurant at Morningside Drive for a smashing meal and a bottle of Mateaus Rose and some good conversation.

1979 Portobello I picked up some messages and petrol. The roads are still quite icy. Mum; John; Yohanan and Áine arrived by taxi early on. Joan; Aunt Dottle; Mum and John went to Darby's funeral in the black hired car whilst Yohanan, Áine and I drove there in Darby's Ford Cortina. Thankfully everything went okay. Later Yohanan and I went up town as with no longer being able to get a lift up to Waverley Station in the early morning with Grandpa Darby I was looking for a bicycle to buy.

1980 Portobello Gavin Miller picked me up at two o'clock and we drove down to Peebles and then out to Lyne Station. Weather-wise it was gloomy with a steady smir of rain. We had tea and scones at the Park Hotel with its marvellous views out across the Borders county valley. By an odd coincidence there was a man of late middle age-early old age also having afternoon tea. When I say coincidence I'd seen him the evening before eating a meal on his own at the Roxburgh Hotel Charlotte Square – a solitary existence which seemed sad. He was a strange mixture – immaculately groomed yet his clothes had seen better days and were slightly shabby but full of good character – his tweed jacket was ripped on one shoulder and along with his waistcoat and baggy trousers he wore a pair of rubbers – an odd juxtaposition. I couldn't but speculate about him; when he went off to the loo he was much smaller than I first thought. Gavin thought he was an old bachelor. On the way back to the capital in the wet and the dark I couldn't but think sadly of Maria and I on that lovely and rather magical summer's day that we spent together in Peebles and then the Ettrick Valley – the game of pool in a little pub; the visit to the potter's shop and of course travelling back to Edinburgh in the snugness, love and warmth of the Triumph Spitfire - the days of wine and roses which I thought formed an unbreakable bond between the two of us. In the evening I ran along a stormy windy Joppa and Portobello esplanade seafront.

1981 Portobello First day back to Napier College and it was tough in Economics. I managed to pass the exam (47%); and Business Finance (56%) and Business Policy (48%) – a high mark as half of our year failed.

1982 Portobello I closed my eyes on the mail train back from London but didn't really sleep at all. The repetitive clickety-clack of wheels on track but bearable as I was looking forward to coming home. I'm a fragile bod. From the Borders onward the landscape was covered in snow. The train arrived at Waverley Station at 6.25 am so I was home to Porty in time for breakfast and a wonderful welcome from Martha as she sat up in bed. The warmth of her welcome and joy of her arms isn't something I'll forget and her delight in seeing me back. Edinburgh was cold and the pavements covered in ice. I ran a light session before meeting Martha for lunch at a lovely intimate little café in Rose Street called Hanky Panky – Spaghetti Bolognese, followed by a Viennese Pancake. We discussed whether I should go to London – that's if I'm offered a job.

1983 Portobello A gloomy morning outwith which reflected my own mood. It was very very windy on my morning run with Steven. As we approached Eastfield we got caught in an icy shower on the long stretch along the Joppa and Portobello seafronts. Running into the wind we could hardly make any headway whatsoever having to keep our heads down; it was so harsh on our pows such was the brain-freeze. After breakfast I took Grandma Joan up to the RSA with three of her paintings. One is a gem; another is good; t'other one is so-so. She's changed her style from flowers, vases and fruit bowls so perhaps it augurs well for a change of luck. Later on I dragged myself up to Duddingston Village and on the border of the Queen's Park did a session on the steps. It was all rather yuck – cold and miserable; the wind was howling and blasting against the trees adjacent to the walled little wynd. There was no-one else around so much so I felt I could be part of any earlier century – fantasies of hill dwellers; loch dwellers; cavemen – Bonnie Prince Charlie could have even ridden up the street en-route to the Sheep's Heid Inn prior to the Battle of Prestonpans – all very strange and surreal. A rather quiet evening in. I've just started reading John Osbourne's autobiography. Whilst in bed reading I heard 'Aunt' Margaret (Ross-Elliot) on the phone to Joan – she begins the removals from 6 Henderson Row Edinburgh to Stobsmills House Gorebridge at 9.30 am tomorrow morning so I'll go and spend the day helping them with the big move.

1984 Powderhall At Oxgangs, Mum, my sister Áine and I were talking about people and the concepts of realism versus romanticism.

1986 Powderhall

Apart
The phone rang.
I wanted it to be you.
It was (Grandma) Joan.
Where had I been?
Is everything all right?
I've not seen you for a week.
I was going to phone your work.
She doesn't know. I've said.
I'll come down at lunchtime.
To see her.
And Probably
Tell her about us.
Apart.
It will worry her.

1987 Morningside Elfin has just telephoned me. She's pregnant! I told Martha the horrendous news at 7.30 pm. She was very supportive. I met Elfin at 8.30 pm at the Canny Man's Morningside. It was slightly unreal – was it all a bad dream? A man with too much to drink sat in a corner telling jokes in a loud voice. I don't know if it was the circumstances but I found them very funny. Elfin was - although not young - I suddenly thought just how young and immature she is. She had nothing really to say about it all just taking it in her stride. Since Martha has been seeing Colin over the past six months I've only gone out with girls on a few occasions sleeping with Elfin twice in the past month or two. She's more or less decided that it would be best not to have the baby. This past year has been a ghastly nightmare, what with Martha seeing Colin again back in the Highlands over Christmas.

Postcard (dated) Tuesday 6th January

Dear Samuel, Thank you for making the beginning of 1987 good for me – somehow I don't think the rest of the year can live up to the first few days – you really have robbed me of my optimism. Just promise me you won't do anything silly - like get married before I move back to Scotland. – or if you do – please don't send me an invitation... These days were pretty short but at the same time it feels like a long long time. I've never felt anything quite quite as right as being with you. Even 3 days is worth having. Emilia Lanier xx P.S. I will write a letter as soon as I have unpacked and sorted some things out – it will probably be awful. Xxxx

1988 Morningside The auditor turned up at work at Danderhall Community Leisure Centre today which was a bit of a surprise. He was of Indian or Pakistani background and quite friendly. Throughout the day we had one or two interesting conversations. He is of the view that the only way to make money is to go into business for yourself. I looked in to see Grandma Joan at lunchtime but no Mum or sister Áine. Joan's into Jeffrey Archer's books just now so, as is her way, she's rattling through the cannon, finding that everything else at home is being left – what a girl (aged 82)!

1989 Morningside Yesterday and today I joined sub 4 minute miler Adrian Weatherhead for some lunchtime runs around the Meadows – quite enjoyable at a conversation pace.

1990 Morningside It's been lovely to hear the birds out singing but have they been fooled by the good weather?

1993 Colinton Martha telephoned me at 9 o'clock to say she had received a call that Janey's (her mum) condition has deteriorated quite quickly so she intends driving up to The Northlands immediately. I telephoned her dad's wife Wyvis's wifey (Martha's step-mother) who said Martha had arrived safely and both Robbie (brother) and Martha would take turns at the bedside. The youngest of her three brothers Bruce (and wife Sheila) left with Sheila's brother Mark for Hawaii and then Australia. Bruce's final parting from Janey's bedside was quite tearful; Martha says that because Janey is on morphine she wasn't too aware of Bruce's imminent departure. Grandma Joan was saying how much she admired Martha's commitment over these past few months. When I visited Janey last week I thought how sad it was to see her finally beaten by the unbeatable, recalling how valiantly and pluckily she had fought off cancer eight years previously and of all she has had to suffer and put up with. Martha phoned me at 9 o'clock in the evening; Janey is pretty much in a coma. She was upset. I told her that I loved her. News came through that Rudolph Nureyev has died.

1994 Colinton Oh well, with it being a Thursday only a two day work after the festive holidays. A miserable atypical January morning. At lunchtime I saw the skin specialist Mr Tidman at his private practice in Edinburgh's New Town. He spent very little time with me. More of the same potions. A certain improvement. 'Your skin is very dry'. Well I could have told him that! I shall be interested to see his bill. He did himself no favours by repeating stories from the previous visitation alongside forgetting personal items about me; if you don't have the memory of an elephant steer clear of such intercourse - it makes the patient feel a nonentity.

1995 Colinton After dinner, although feeling tired I realised I had to clear out our downstairs bedroom to accommodate my friend Tristan's imminent arrival (temporary split from his wife and children). Martha and I managed to fill up two sacks of ephemera to dump - one positive outcome; it's given him plenty of space to hang up his clothes.

*'Down with the rosemary, and so
Down with the bays and misletoe ;
Down with the holly, ivy, all,
Wherewith ye dress'd the Christmas Hall :
That so the superstitious find
No one least branch there left behind :
For look, how many leaves there be
Neglected, there (maids, trust to me)
So many goblins you shall see...'*

Robert Herrick

Printed in Great Britain
by Amazon

cc4b3b90-e298-4656-a8af-37d642ed9116R01